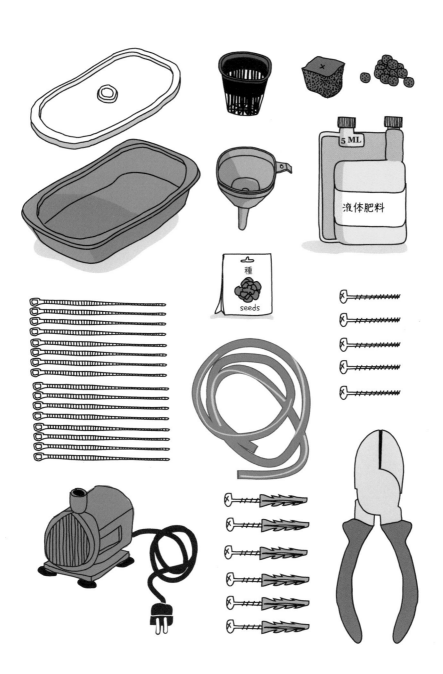

ELIOOO

How to go to IKEA® and build a device to grow food in your apartment.

ANTONIO SCARPONI

3rdO books

Published by Third O Books

3rd**O**

Hermetschloostrasse 70 #2.16 Zurich, 8048, Switzerland.
www.3rdo.com

ISBN 978-3-9524132-8-9

This book was realized with the support of IKEA Switzerland and many, many
other people thanks to a successful crowdfunding campaign via @indiegogo,
made in 2013.

Antonio Scarponi (@scarponio) is an architect and designer. He is the founder of **[onceptual)evices**, a research and development office for design and architecture.
He studied architecture at Cooper Union, New York and at IUAV University, Venice, from which he holds a PhD in Urban Design.
In 2008 he was one of the five recipients of the Curry Stone Design Prize, and in 2012 he was nominated for the Katerva Sustainability Award.

www.conceptualdevices.com

TABLE OF CONTENTS

FOREWORD   11

A PROCESS THAT I CALL RESEARCH   13
Or How this Project Came to Be

A LONG WAY TO SAY THANK YOU   17
Acknowledgements

THE FIVE DESIGN PROBLEMS FOR WORKING WITH HYDROPONICS   21

    1   SEEDLINGS   23
    2   CONTAINERS   36
    3   OXYGEN   41
    4   NUTRIENT SOLUTION   45
    5   LIGHT   54

ELIOOO *Grow Your Food*   59

    ELIOOO #4   61
    ELIOOO #8   69
    ELIOOO #Desk   80
    ELIOOO #30   99
    ELIOOO #30 Mobile   117
    ELIOOO #30 Mobile off grid   143

AFTERWARD   151

THE SLAP MANAGEMENT MODEL *Notes For A Manifesto*   153
By Adrian Notz

FOREWORD

BY FOLLOWING THE INSTRUCTIONS IN THIS BOOK, YOU WILL BECOME THE MANUFACTURER OF AN IDEA.

THIS BOOK IS AN INSTRUCTION MANUAL FOR A PRODUCT THAT ONLY EXISTS IF YOU BUILD IT. HERE ARE THE INSTRUCTIONS. I HAVE DESIGNED THIS DEVICE SO THAT YOU CAN PRODUCE YOUR OWN FOOD USING SOME INEXPENSIVE IKEA BOXES, SOME BASIC GARDENING MATERIAL, AND THE DIRECTIONS IN THIS BOOK.

THIS SYSTEM USES HYDROPONICS, A FARMING TECHNIQUE THAT CAN BE USED TO GROW PLANTS IN WATER INSTEAD OF SOIL. THE REASON FOR USING HYDROPONICS IS VERY SIMPLE: IT ALLOWS YOU TO SAVE UP TO THE 90% OF THE WATER USED IN TRADITIONAL AGRICULTURE SYSTEMS, REQUIRES MUCH LESS SPACE, AND YOU DON'T HAVE TO WORRY ABOUT WATERING THE PLANTS.

THE SYSTEM THAT I HAVE DESIGNED COMBINES DIFFERENT TECHNIQUES, ADAPTED TO MAKE THIS EASY TO DO AT HOME, TURNING YOU INTO A FARMER, PERHAPS AN URBAN FARMER. HOWEVER THIS BOOK IS NOT A BOOK ON URBAN FARMING, NOR IS IT A GENERAL BOOK ABOUT HYDROPONICS. THIS BOOK IS A MANUAL THAT WILL SHOW YOU HOW TO BUILD AND RUN A SIMPLE HYDROPONIC SYSTEM WITH SOME INEXPENSIVE IKEA BOXES. I CALL THIS SYSTEM ELI000.

I BELIEVE THAT THE ULTIMATE OBJECT OF DESIGN IS KNOWLEDGE. AS A DESIGNER, I VISUALIZE QUANTITIES AND DIMENSIONS, I ORGANIZE BRIEFS, I EXPLAIN PROCEDURES. SOMETIMES THIS HAS MORE TO DO WITH STORYTELLING THAN WITH TECHNICAL DRAWINGS. THESE STORIES AND THEIR ILLUSTRATIONS ARE TRADITIONALLY GIVEN TO ARTISANS WHO TURN THEM INTO CONCRETE THINGS. BUT AS A DESIGNER, I LIKE TO DESIGN THINGS THAT ANYONE CAN MAKE. TODAY DESIGN CAN TURN THE WORLD'S POPULATION INTO THE BIGGEST CREATIVE INDUSTRY EVER KNOWN: A CROWD FACTORY. RATHER THAN MINDLESSLY PRODUCING NEW STUFF, DISTRIBUTING IT, AND REINVENTING NEW PRODUCTION AND DISTRIBUTION CHAINS, I THINK WE SHOULD FIND NEW WAYS OF ASSEMBLING WHAT WE ALREADY HAVE.
FOR THIS REASON, I DECIDED TO DESIGN ELI000 USING ITEMS FROM IKEA. EVERYBODY KNOWS WHERE TO FIND AN IKEA STORE AND HOW MUCH THE ITEMS WILL COST.

BUT THE GOAL OF DESIGN IS ALSO TO INSPIRE. ELI000 IS DESIGNED SO THAT YOU CAN PLAY AROUND WITH THE DIFFERENT SETUPS I SUGGEST IN THE BOOK, WITH OR WITHOUT THE USE OF IKEA COMPONENTS.

TINKER WITH THE CONFIGURATIONS, TWEAK THE SYSTEM, PLAY WITH THE SETUP, BUILD SOMETHING. BE INVENTIVE. GROW YOUR FOOD.

ENJOY IT.

A. S.

A PROCESS THAT I CALL
RESEARCH *Or How This Project Came To Be*

This book has a fairly long story. It is the result of a process that I call research. I do many projects of this kind. I have used IKEA items before in my work. The first time was in 2008 for a competition in Turin launched by ABITARE (@abitare), an Italian Design Magazine, which at the time was directed by the architect Stefano Boeri (@StefanoBoeri), on *geodesign*. The idea was to connect local communities, designers, and corporations to produce site-specific prototypes to address specific needs of specific communities. Marco Lampugnani (@mlampu) and I applied to this competition. We chose to reorganize a flea market. Our proposal was accepted and we ran workshops with the volunteer organization that organized the market. We were told that this is one of the poorest flea markets in Europe. Our job was to mark each merchant's allotted space, build a foldable trolley used to deliver goods to the space, and build a temporary rain and sun shelter. After a discussion with Lucia Tozzi, one of the editors of ABITARE, we were able to secure some technical sponsorship from IKEA in Italy thanks to Valerio di Bussolo, the Italian Public Relations Manager. This allowed us to build the entire project out of items from IKEA. We called this project RIKEA, and were invited to present it at the Architecture Biennale in Rotterdam in 2009 where we received an honorable mention.

A few months later, I was asked to be part of an editorial project curated by Pedro Gadanho (@pedrogadanho). He asked me to write a science fiction story about "scenarios and speculations" of the future of the city for a new book series called *Beyond*. I wrote a story about this amazing flea market. I imagined a world in which all the resources had been used up, replaced with already manufactured items. In this world, design was information, a form of knowledge that was necessary in order to make anything, and design was a practice that reorganized uninformed matter over and over again, each time in a different way. This was the core idea behind RIKEA.

Later, in 2011, I had the chance to develop another sort of science fiction project. This time, it was a device to grow fish and vegetables in a combined unit. It was developed as a side project of a commission I had from a Startup called UrbanFarmers for an aquaponic farm for a rooftop in Basel, Switzerland. Again, I used IKEA parts. In order to find out more about how aquaponic farming works, I decided to run a research project to see how much food could be produced in a normal apartment. Andreas Graber, co-founder of UrbanFarmers helped me to define the farming specs of a prototype I wanted to build. I designed a device that I called *Malthus, a meal a day. Malthus* is able to grow 200g of fish (a portion) and a portion of salad a day. With a little irony, I was referring to Robert Malthus who, in his book *An Essay on the Principle of Population* (1798) claimed: "The power of population is indefinitely greater than the power in the Earth to produce subsistence for man." Before him, nobody had questioned the capacity of the Earth's resources to sustain its inhabitants. The question is still wide open and I wanted to engage with it with this piece which was financed with the help of some resources from an exhibition curated by Po Hagström called *Power Landscapes* in Stockholm. This was the seed that made me grow sprouts in my office.

As a designer, I give ideas a form and I transform them into concrete things. I certainly can't solve the world's problems, but what I can do is to create a narrative about them. This is where the ideas and thoughts behind ELIOOO come from. But the idea for ELIOOO itself was conceived after an exhibition I was asked to design for the Cabaret Voltaire, the DADA house, in Zurich. The exhibition was called *DADA New York II: Revolution to Smash Global Capitalism* and featured the artists The Yes Men, Reverend Billy, and Voina. Since being "apolitical" is itself a strong political statement, design is my own form of activism. I decided to play with the irony of the idea that to smash capitalism, one needs capitalism.

The choice to use only IKEA items to design the exhibition came after. The idea was to assemble an installation that could be returned to the store after the show closed three-months later, in accordance with IKEA's customer satisfaction service policy. I wanted to design an exhibition that could be replicated anywhere in the world, by simply going to the IKEA store to collect the materials. This way, the exhibition could be replicated nearly anywhere at a very limited cost. The exhibition space was designed as a combination of a "headquarters," a concept store, and a workshop space. With three items - storage boxes (Trofast), a bookshelf system (Antonius), and zip ties, I furnished the space with everything you could possibly need: a bed, lamps, a bedside table, three large bookshelves, two workshop tables, some stools, an armchair, and even a sofa. Together with Adrian Notz and Philip Meier, we decided to call this installation *Readykea*. It was by far the cheapest exhibition ever to be installed at Cabaret Voltaire.

A couple of months later, Susanna Legrenzi, Stefano Mirti, and Marco Patroni invited me to participate in a one night exhibition called *Foster Care* during the Salone del Mobile in Milano. I decided to add a new element to the *Readykea* Collection, a hydroponic device to grow food. There, I presented *Zoroaster*, which is now called ELIOOO #30. After this exhibition, I realized that I could make a whole bunch of different hydroponic devices with these same elements. I decided to contact IKEA to ask for sponsorship. I explained my plans to run a crowdfunding campaign to support the writing, illustration, and production of a book (this one) which I could offer to my supporters as a perk. Once again, they stepped in.

A LONG WAY TO SAY
THANK YOU - *Acknowledgements*

This story is a long way to thank all the people who have helped me along the way. A project like this could not have happened without this back story and the generosity of the people who helped me make it happen. David Affentrager is doing great work at IKEA Switzerland. He is one of those rare people who does what he says he will do. And I could not even imagine doing a crowdfunding campaign without the brainstorming meetings with @_____thenomad and Jimena Quintana and the great text editing and crowdfunding advice from Amber Hickey. I also have to thank Monica Tarocco (@moniemmeti), Carlo Pisani (@carlopisani), and Eleonora Stassi (@eleonora_sta), for taking pictures of the prototypes during the early stages of the work, before presenting ELIOOO at the Salone in Milano, Italy.
My deepest gratitude goes to Stefano Massa (@doctorcrowd), who worked with me here at Conceptual Devices, solving all sorts of problems. He is the master behind the crowdfunding campaign video and the CSS coding of the ELIOOO website. In addition to this, I owe him a lot as a friend, for his great patience, and as a collaborator, for the many projects we have been working on together at Conceptual Devices. A big thank you goes to Tido Von Oppeln who helped me frame this book within some of the key challenges of contemporary design. And even a greater one to Liz Henry (@whereareyouliz) from Nuance Words. Liz helped me many times by editing text for projects I was trying to write. Writing is a very difficult job, especially if you happen to write in a language that it is not your own, like I am doing now. I always have the feeling of walking in a dark crowded room. I am always afraid of stepping on someone's foot. Liz helped me find my way. Amber Hickey double checked that.

I also want to thank the crowd who supported this book. Without these people, this project would not have been possible. These are amazing people, who supported the concept of a book that turns individuals into the manufacturers of an idea, before seeing it finished. These people are not only conceptual manufacturers, they are also producers, facilitators, sponsors and ultimately, the amplifiers of this idea. They helped me make this idea tangible. A very special thanks to: Alberto Gascon, Aldo Mazola, Ally Motorcade, Andrea Botto, Andrea Zausa, Andreas Schmeil, Anna Barbara, Attilio Barzaghi, August Flassig, Boonkai Lee, Chin Yi Chieng, Chris Amos, Chris Niewiarowski, Christian Langenegger, Claudia Meier, Claudio Farina, Cristina Perillo, Cristina Senatore, Daniel Frei, Daniela Bettoni, Danika Hadgraft, David Schneller, David Van Berckel, Davide Sacconi, Deanna Brown, Elisa Ossino, Eric Damon Walters, Evelyn Leveghi, Felix Kuestahler, Frederick Wells, Giacomo Pirazzoli, Gianluigi D'Angelo, Gillard Magalie, Gioia Guerzoni, Greg Perkins, Janelle Wohltmann, Jeremy Hulette, Joyce Miletic, Julia Graf, Karen Smith, Kaspar Manz, Kate Hofman, Kimball Finigan, Koen Verschaeren, Laura Basco, Lisa Asmussen, Lisa Rempp, Louis Silverman, Lucia Giuliano, Magnus Dahlstrand, Maria Costea, Mariano Dallago, Marina Metaxa, Mario Cantarella, Marius Finnstun, Mark Durno, Martin Locher, Martin Pfaundler, Mathew Kinghorn, Maurizio Cilli, Melanie Gajowski, Michael Keller, Natascia Fenoglio, Nathan Wolf, Nicole Sauvageau, Olle Lundell, Pablo Castillo, Pamela Ferri, Paolo Priolo, Paul Fields, Phillip Frankland, Rachele Storai, Rebecca De Marchi, Rebecca Defoe, Robert Mason, Samuele Anzellotti, Simona Galateo, Stefan Hornke, Stefan Leijon, Stefano Mirti, Steve Swiggers, Stewart Adams, Susanna Legrenzi, Tammy Johnson, Taroh Kogure, Taylor Banks, Thalia Lehmann, Tieme Van Veen,

Vincent Uher, Walter Nicolino, Younjin Kim, and the many others who preferred to remain anonymous. Many thanks to two big supporters, my first two resellers: Veg and the City (@Veg_andthecity) and Nerd Communications (@nerdcomms), as well as to the many, many people who pre-ordered this book on www.eliooo.com while it was being developed and since our crowdfunding campaign.

Creating a successful crowdfunding campaign is very hard work and often this alone is not enough - you also need a lot of luck. I worked really hard for this project but I was also very lucky. This campaign was supported by amazing people, my friends. Thanks to Daniel Frei (@da_frei), for all the support and advice. In one word, thank you for your friendship.
A big thank you to Remo Ricchetti (@remo_ricchetti) who suggested using the perverse tactic of the birthday on FB as marketing. Thank you to Stefano Mirti (@stefi_idlab) for taking this idea seriously and encouraging the brilliant motto of "support this project and get something for yourself" on the FB page *Gran Touristas* (@GranTouristas) that he created together with Remo, and Daniele Mancini as a social media project for the Italian Pavilion at the Venice Architecture Biennale 2012.

I also want to mention the people who talked about this project in their blogs and social media channels and helped it spread across the internet. Thanks to Tina Roth Eisenberg (@swissmiss), Maria Popova (@brainpicker), who covered this project in the last few days of my campaign and contributed to the final push, to Jennifer Hattam (@jenhattam) and to Sumandro Chattapadhyay (@ajantriks) for writing very nice and accurate articles for the respective blogs they write for: *Treehugger* and *Pop-up City*.

Lastly, I want to thank my wife Phaedra for the ground funding of this and the many other projects I am engaged in with her support, which is called life. This book is dedicated to our daughter with the hope that one day we can go through these pages together and laugh about what a crazy father she has.

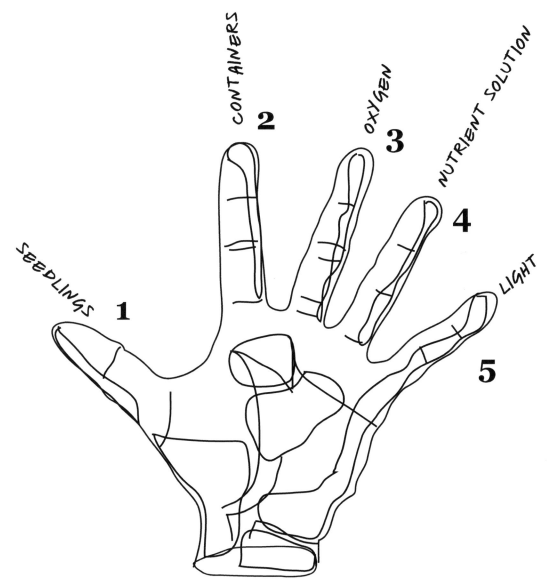

CONTAINERS **2**

OXYGEN **3**

NUTRIENT SOLUTION **4**

SEEDLINGS **1**

LIGHT **5**

THE FIVE DESIGN PROBLEMS FOR WORKING WITH HYDROPONICS

SOIL, IN AGRICULTURE IS AN EXCUSE. PLANTS DO NOT HAVE TO BE STUCK IN THE GROUND. HYDROPONICS IS A FARMING TECHNIQUE THAT ALLOWS YOU TO GROW PLANTS IN WATER, GIVEN THAT YOU PROVIDE THE NECESSARY NOURISHMENT AND OXYGEN TO THE ROOTS.

TECHNICALLY SPEAKING, SOIL HAS TWO ROLES. THE FIRST IS TO SUPPORT THE PLANT SO IT CAN GROW UPWARDS. THE SECOND IS TO PROVIDE NUTRIENTS AND OXYGEN TO IT. AS ORGANIC MATTER DECOMPOSES, IT FREES UP PURE ELEMENTS FOR THE PLANT TO USE AS NOURISHMENT. OXYGEN CAN BE FOUND IN THE AIR CONTAINED IN THE SOIL. IF THE SOIL IS COMPACT AND RICH, LIKE – SAY – CLAY, THERE WOULD BE NEARLY NO CHANCE FOR PLANTS TO GROW BECAUSE THERE WOULD NOT BE ENOUGH OXYGEN FOR THE ROOTS. IF THE NUTRIENTS ARE ADDED DIRECTLY TO THE WATER, THE ROOTS CAN TAKE CARE OF THE REST, UNDER THE CONDITION THAT YOU PROVIDE THEM WITH THE NECESSARY OXYGEN SO THAT THEY CAN BREATHE.

WITH HYDROPONICS YOU CAN SAVE UP TO 90% OF THE WATER OTHERWISE NEEDED FOR TRADITIONAL SOIL–BASED FARMING SYSTEMS. IT ALLOWS YOU TO GROW MORE PLANTS IN LESS SPACE. IT PREVENTS THE DIFFUSION OF PESTS, FUNGI, AND OTHER DISEASES THAT CAN BE FOUND IN THE SOIL. IT ELIMINATES THE PRESENCE OF WEEDS (THEREFORE THERE IS NO NEED FOR HERBICIDES). THE TURNAROUND TIME BETWEEN PLANTING IS REDUCED AS NO SOIL PREPARATION IS REQUIRED AND YOU DO NOT HAVE TO WATER THE PLANTS.

WORKING WITH HYDROPONICS MEANS THAT YOU HAVE TO FACE FIVE DESIGN PROBLEMS IN ORDER TO ENJOY ITS BENEFITS. IN THIS BOOK I HAVE DEVELOPED A SYSTEM IN WHICH I SUGGEST SOLUTIONS FOR HOW TO SOLVE THEM. I DO THIS BY USING SOME ITEMS FROM IKEA AND SOME RATHER STANDARD GARDENING EQUIPMENT. EL1000 IS ALL ABOUT THE SPATIAL SOLUTION OF THESE FIVE HYDROPONIC PROBLEMS.
THERE ARE ENDLESS WAYS TO SOLVE THEM. EL1000 IS THE MOST SIMPLE ONE I COULD DEVELOP USING INEXPENSIVE ELEMENTS AVAILABLE NEARLY EVERYWHERE.

1

SEEDLINGS

IT IS VERY IMPORTANT THAT YOU START THE
SEEDLINGS YOURSELF. THIS IS BECAUSE YOU WILL
BE ABLE TO KNOW EXACTLY WHERE YOUR PLANT
IS COMING FROM AND YOU CAN SENSIBLY REDUCE
THE POSSIBILITY OF SPREADING PESTS IN YOUR
SYSTEM.

THERE ARE TWO WAYS TO START A SEEDLING.
THE FIRST IS TO PLANT A SEED IN A GROW
STARTER (MEDIUM) THAT WILL HELP THE SEED
SPROUT. THE SECOND IS TO CLONE YOUR
FAVOURITE PLANT INTO A NEW, IDENTICAL ONE.

THESE ARE THE ELEMENTS YOU NEED TO GROW SEEDLINGS:

A

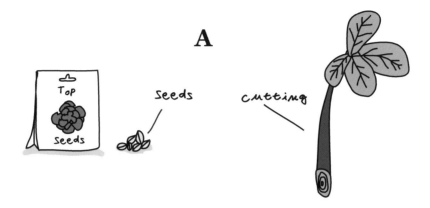

HOW TO OBTAIN A SEEDLING FROM A SEED OR FROM A CUTTING
WILL BE EXPLAINED IN THE NEXT FEW PAGES.

B

THESE ARE TYPICALLY BLACK AND ALLOW THE ROOTS TO GROW
INTO THE WATER. FOR THIS SYSTEM, I RECOMMEND USING THE
SMALLER ONES WHICH ARE ABOUT 5 CM.

THE NET POTS CAN ALSO BE D.I.Y.ED.
SMALL YOGURT CUPS WORK FINE. JUST MAKE SURE TO DRILL A
LOT OF HOLES SO THAT THE ROOTS CAN GROW INTO THE
WATER.

C

STARTER MEDIUM

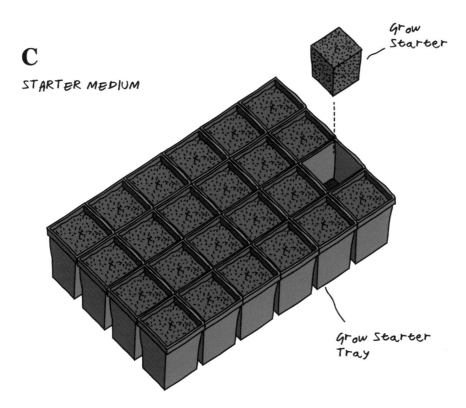

Grow Starter

Grow Starter Tray

THERE ARE MANY TYPES OF STARTER MEDIUMS. I RECOMMEND THE ONE MADE OF COCONUT FIBRES AND ORGANIC COMPOST THAT ARE MOLDED IN A POLYMER BINDER. I LIKE THEM BECAUSE THEY ARE MADE OF ORGANIC MATERIAL AND MAKE TRANSPLANTATION EASIER AS THEY DO NOT BREAK APART WHEN YOU PULL THEM OUT OF THEIR PLASTIC TRAY INSERTS. THEY ALSO DIRECT THE ROOTS DOWNWARDS, SO THAT THEY CAN GROW INTO THE FERTILIZED WATER MORE EASILY AFTER TRANSPLANTATION. THEY COME IN DIFFERENT SIZES AND FORMS. JUST MAKE SURE THEY MATCH WITH THE 5 CM NET POTS, OR WHATEVER SIZE YOU CHOOSE TO USE.

D

Expanded clay

LIGHTWEIGHT EXPANDED CLAY AGGREGATE (LECA) IS A PERFECT STARTER MEDIUM. IT SUPPORTS THE PLANT STRUCTURALLY, LIKE SOIL DOES. THIS IS MY FAVOURITE MEDIUM BECAUSE IT IS INEXPENSIVE, PH NEUTRAL, LIGHTWEIGHT, AND EASY TO FIND. THE ONLY CAUTION IS THAT IF YOU ARE USING PUMPS IN YOUR SYSTEM, YOU WANT TO RINSE THE LECA WITH WATER BEFORE USING IT TO GET RID OF ANY SMALL PARTICLES THAT MIGHT DAMAGE THE EQUIPMENT. OTHER MEDIUMS THAT CAN BE USED IN HYDROPONICS ARE: PERLITE, COCONUT COIR, AND ROCKWOOL.

PLANTING SEEDS

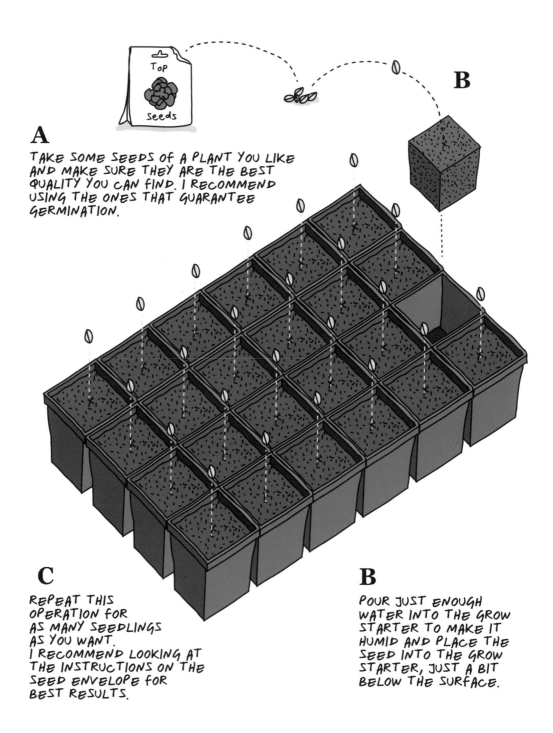

A

TAKE SOME SEEDS OF A PLANT YOU LIKE AND MAKE SURE THEY ARE THE BEST QUALITY YOU CAN FIND. I RECOMMEND USING THE ONES THAT GUARANTEE GERMINATION.

B

POUR JUST ENOUGH WATER INTO THE GROW STARTER TO MAKE IT HUMID AND PLACE THE SEED INTO THE GROW STARTER, JUST A BIT BELOW THE SURFACE.

C

REPEAT THIS OPERATION FOR AS MANY SEEDLINGS AS YOU WANT. I RECOMMEND LOOKING AT THE INSTRUCTIONS ON THE SEED ENVELOPE FOR BEST RESULTS.

D

PLACE THE GROW STARTER TRAY
INSIDE THE MINI GREENHOUSE
AND VAPORIZE SOME WATER
TO KEEP IT MOIST.
YOU CAN GET ONE
IN A GARDENING SHOP.
OTHERWISE A PLASTIC BAG
COULD ALSO WORK.

E

PLACE THE
COVER ON TOP
OF IT AND POSITION
THE GREENHOUSE
IN A WARM AND
BRIGHT PLACE WITH
INDIRECT LIGHT.

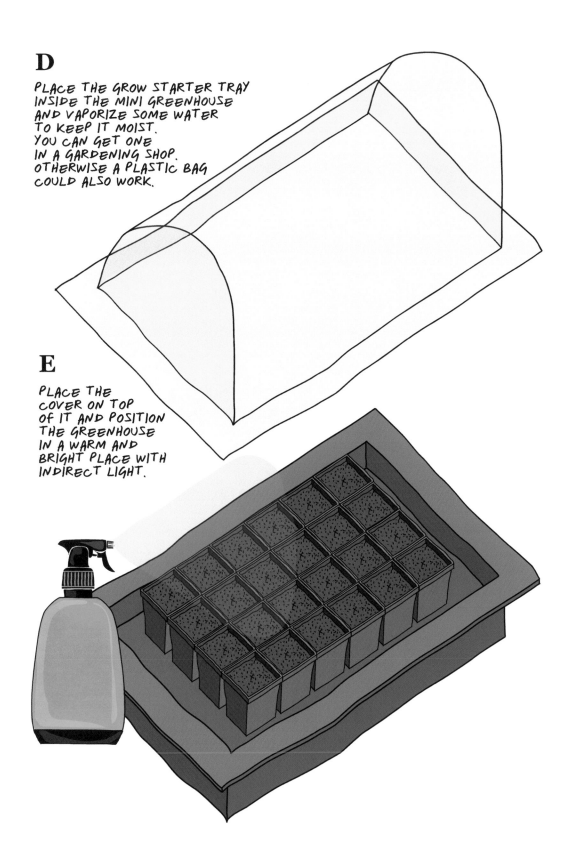

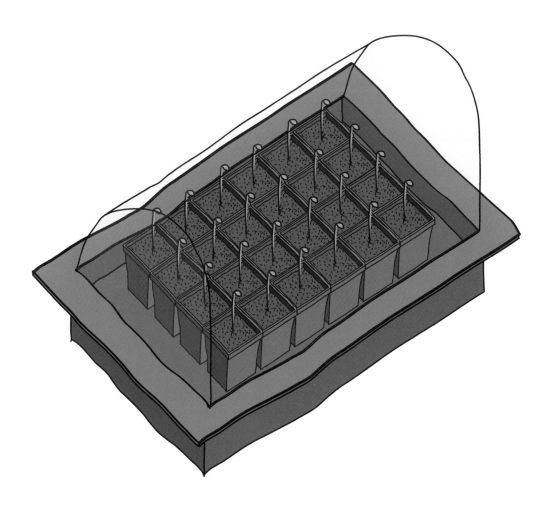

F

AFTER A FEW DAYS, THE SEEDS MIGHT START TO SPROUT. NOW, ALL YOU NEED TO DO IS KEEP THE GROW STARTER HUMID AND WARM.

WHEN THEY START TO GROW, MOVE THE SEEDLINGS TO BRIGHTER LIGHT. WHEN THEY START TO DEVELOP SOME PROPER LEAVES, YOU CAN REMOVE THE COVER. IT'S ESSENTIAL THAT YOU KEEP THE GROW STARTER MOIST, BUT NOT SOAKED.

G

AS SOON AS THE SEEDS TURN INTO SEEDLINGS WITH ONE OR TWO ROUNDS OF LEAVES, IT IS TIME TO TRANSPLANT THEM INTO YOUR HYDROPONIC SYSTEM. LIFT THE SEEDLING AND STARTER GENTLY, TAKING CARE NOT TO DAMAGE THE ROOTS.

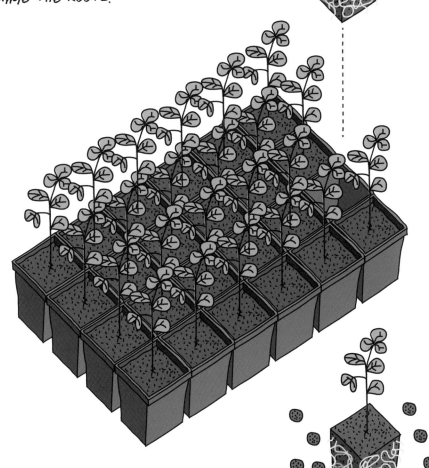

H

PLACE EACH SEEDLING INTO A NET POT AND FILL THE GAPS WITH SOME EXPANDED CLAY. MAKE SURE THE GROW STARTERS REMAIN MOIST UNTIL THE ROOTS GROW TO REACH THE WATER. CONGRATULATIONS — A NEW PLANT IS GROWING.

CLONING

PLANTS CAN BE CLONED. THERE ARE MANY WAYS TO GROW PLANTS, AND CLONING IS SURELY ONE OF THE MOST EFFICIENT. IT ALLOWS YOU TO SAVE A LOT OF TIME BY COPYING YOUR FAVOURITE PLANT WITHOUT THE HASSLE OF GROWING FROM SEED. TO CLONE A PLANT IS SIMPLE. THIS IS WHAT YOU NEED:

ROOTING HORMONE TO ACCELERATE THE DEVELOPMENT OF THE ROOTS.

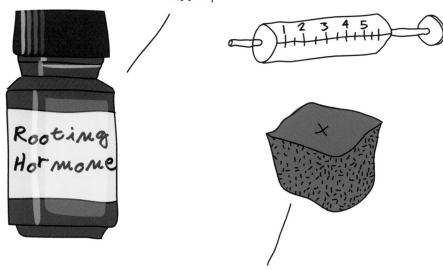

GROW STARTER TO PLACE THE BRANCH THAT ALLOWS FOR ROOT DEVELOPMENT.

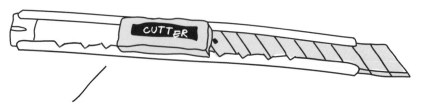

SHARP AND STERILE BLADE TO CUT THE PLANT THAT YOU WANT TO CLONE.

HOW TO PROCEED

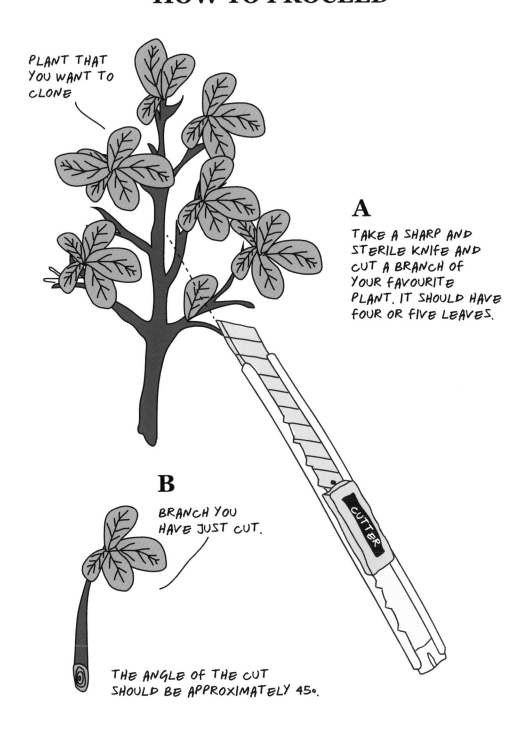

PLANT THAT
YOU WANT TO
CLONE

A

TAKE A SHARP AND
STERILE KNIFE AND
CUT A BRANCH OF
YOUR FAVOURITE
PLANT. IT SHOULD HAVE
FOUR OR FIVE LEAVES.

CUTTER

B

BRANCH YOU
HAVE JUST CUT.

THE ANGLE OF THE CUT
SHOULD BE APPROXIMATELY 45°.

EXTRA CUT
TO PREVENT
EMBOLISM.

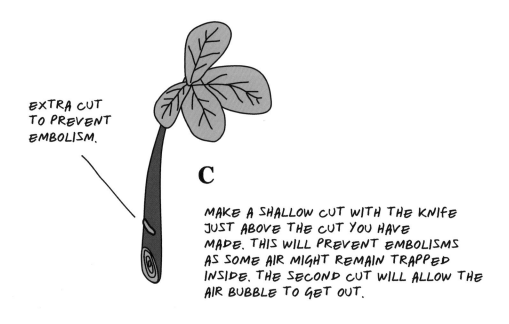

C

MAKE A SHALLOW CUT WITH THE KNIFE
JUST ABOVE THE CUT YOU HAVE
MADE. THIS WILL PREVENT EMBOLISMS
AS SOME AIR MIGHT REMAIN TRAPPED
INSIDE. THE SECOND CUT WILL ALLOW THE
AIR BUBBLE TO GET OUT.

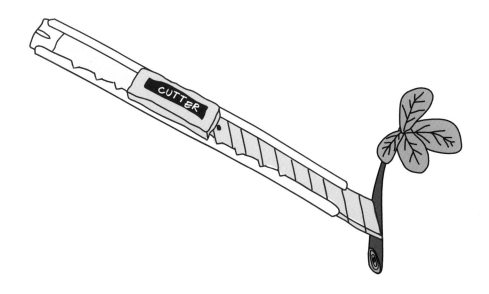

CUTTER

D

WITH A STERILE SYRINGE, TAKE SOME
HORMONES.

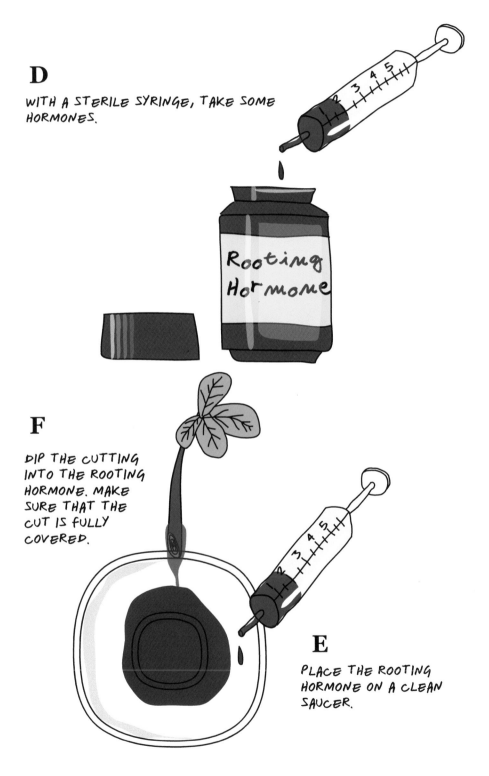

F

DIP THE CUTTING
INTO THE ROOTING
HORMONE. MAKE
SURE THAT THE
CUT IS FULLY
COVERED.

E

PLACE THE ROOTING
HORMONE ON A CLEAN
SAUCER.

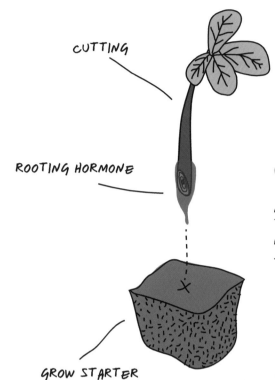

CUTTING

ROOTING HORMONE

GROW STARTER

G

NOW YOU CAN INSERT THE BRANCH INTO A HUMIDIFIED GROW STARTER.

H

NOW MAKE SURE TO KEEP THE BRANCH IN INDIRECT SUNLIGHT IN A WARM AND HUMID ENVIRONMENT UNTIL THE ROOTS GROW OUTSIDE THE STARTER. YOU CAN ALSO COVER IT WITH A TRANSPARENT LID TO MAINTAIN THE LEVEL OF HUMIDITY. THE IDEA IS THAT YOU HAVE A SORT OF MINI GREENHOUSE. VAPORIZE SOME WATER FROM TIME TO TIME AND KEEP THE STARTER HUMID. AS IT GROWS, MOVE THE BRANCH GRADUALLY INTO STRONGER SUNLIGHT.

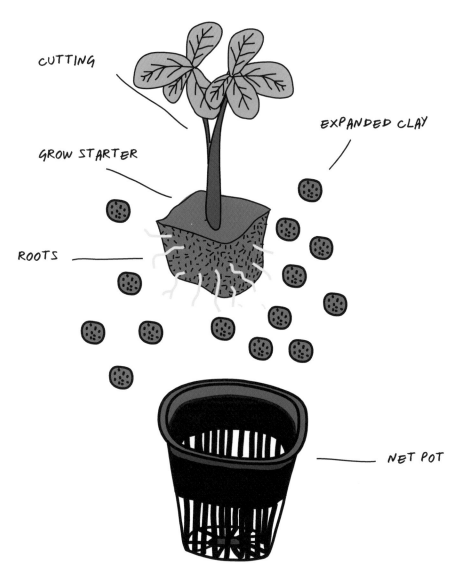

CUTTING

EXPANDED CLAY

GROW STARTER

ROOTS

NET POT

I

INSERT THE GROW STARTER
INTO THE NET POT AND FILL
THE GAPS WITH THE EXPANDED
CLAY. YOUR PLANT IS NOW READY
TO GROW IN YOUR ELI000
SYSTEM.

2

problem

CONTAINERS

TO GROW PLANTS IN THIS HYDROPONIC SYSTEM, YOU NEED A CONTAINER. IN ORDER TO MAKE THINGS SIMPLE, I SUGGEST YOU USE THE TROFAST BOXES PRODUCED BY IKEA. WHY? BECAUSE THEY ARE COLOURFUL, THE COST IS MINIMAL AND THEY ARE AVAILABLE IN DIFFERENT SIZES. THEY ALSO HAVE MATCHING WHITE LIDS THAT REFLECT THE LIGHT THAT CAN BE CUT TO FIT THE NET POTS, AND LAST BUT NOT LEAST, ALL THE PLASTIC PRODUCED BY IKEA FOLLOWS A STRICT BPA-FREE POLICY.

501.158.62

I PREFER TO USE THE COLORED TROFAST BUCKETS BECAUSE THEY CAN SHIELD THE LIGHT BETTER AND PREVENT THE FORMATION OF ALGAE. ALGAE ALSO LIKES FERTILIZER, BUT THE FERTILIZER SHOULD ONLY BE FOR YOUR PLANTS.

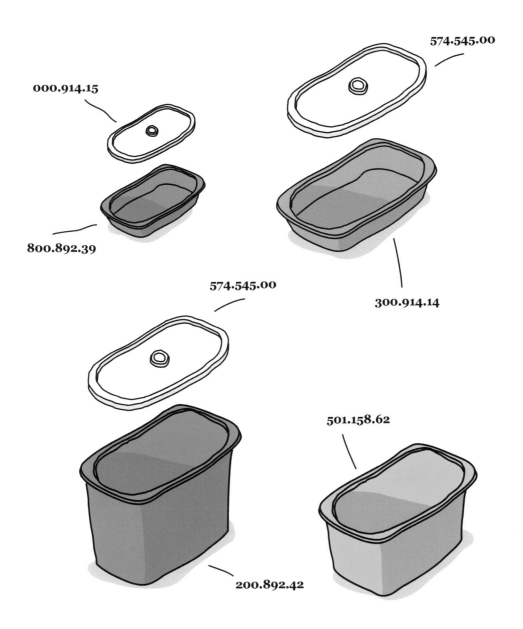

000.914.15

574.545.00

800.892.39

574.545.00

300.914.14

501.158.62

200.892.42

FOR MAXIMUM USE OF SPACE, I RECOMMEND INSTALLING EIGHT
POTS IN EACH CONTAINER. HOWEVER YOU MIGHT WANT TO GIVE
THE PLANTS MORE SPACE TO GROW, DEPENDING ON THE TYPE OF
PLANT. MAKE SURE YOU KNOW HOW MUCH SPACE EACH KIND OF
PLANT NEEDS TO GROW. YOU CAN ALWAYS MOVE THE PLANTS IF
THEY OUTGROW THE CONTAINERS.

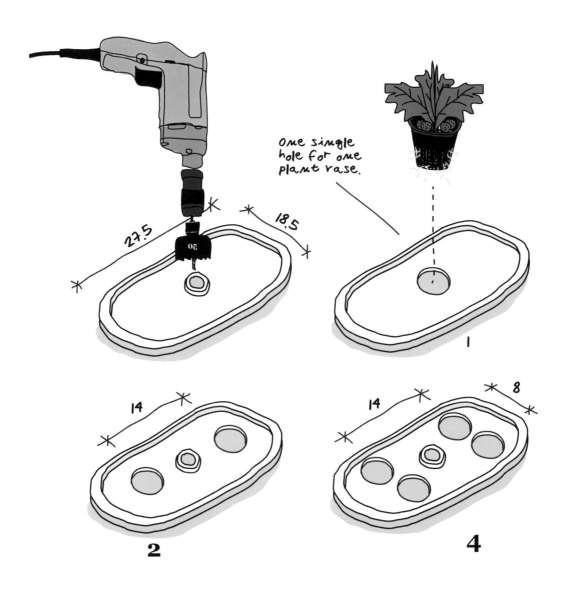

one single
hole for one
plant rase.

27.5

18.5

20

1

14

2

14

8

4

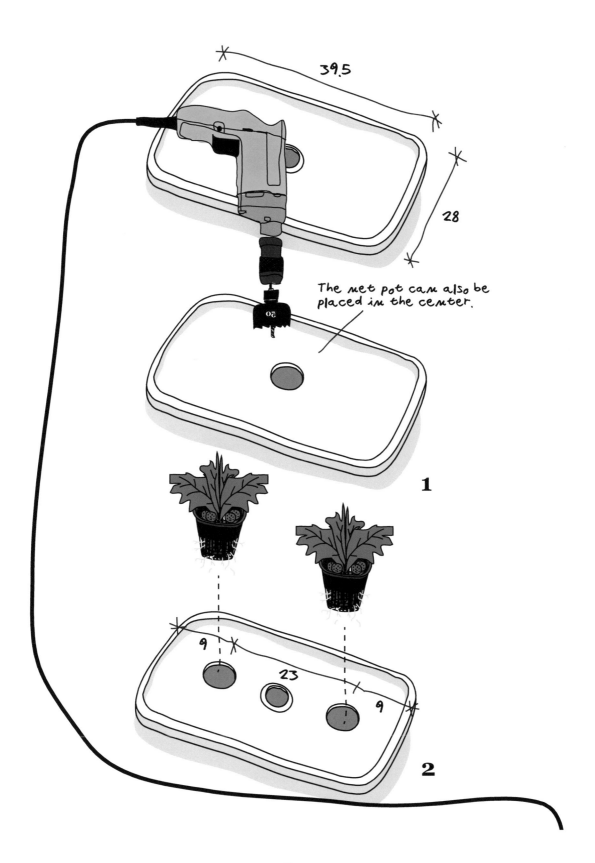

39.5

28

The net pot can also be placed in the center.

1

9

23

9

2

39

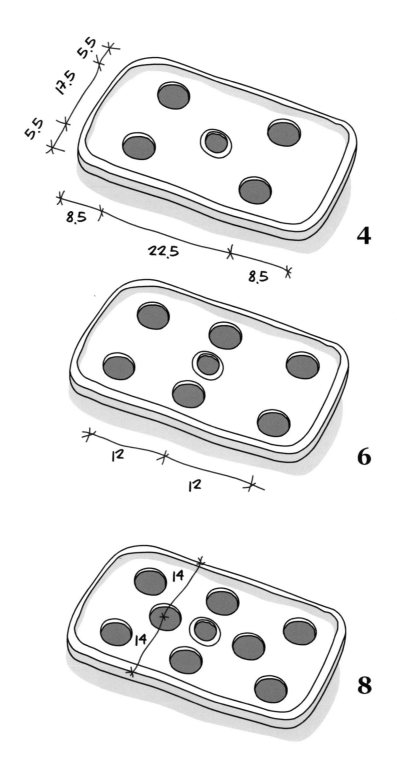

4

6

8

3

NUTRIENT SOLUTION AKA FERTILIZE!

THIS IS TYPICALLY DONE WITH THE USE OF FERTILIZERS. FERTILIZERS ARE PURE ELEMENTS OR MACRO-NUTRIENTS DISSOLVED IN WATER. THERE ARE MANY DIFFERENT KINDS AVAILABLE TO BUY. YOU COULD ALSO MAKE THEM YOURSELF. FOR THE PURPOSE OF THIS BOOK I RECOMMEND TRYING TO GET THE BEST QUALITY FERTILIZER AVAILABLE. ASK IN A GARDENING SHOP ABOUT "HYDROPONIC FERTILIZERS" AND YOU SHOULD BE DIRECTED TO THE RIGHT PRODUCT. ON THE INTERNET, YOU CAN FIND ALL SORTS OF OTHER OPTIONS AND INSTRUCTIONS FOR DIYERS. JUST BE AWARE THAT MOST FERTILIZERS ARE DESIGNED FOR SOFT WATER, MEANING WATER WITH A LOW PERCENTAGE OF MINERALS. THIS IS THE MOST COMMON WATER AVAILABLE IN WATER PIPE INFRASTRUCTURE IN URBAN ENVIRONMENTS. THERE ARE PRODUCTS DESIGNED FOR HARD WATER. IF YOU ARE UNSURE, ASK YOUR WATER COMPANY ABOUT WHETHER YOUR WATER IS HARD OR SOFT. THEN YOU CAN GET THE RIGHT FERTILIZER FOR IT. I ASSUME THAT IF YOU ASK IN YOUR LOCAL GARDENING SHOP, THEY WOULD ALSO KNOW WHETHER THE WATER IN YOUR TOWN IS HARD OR SOFT.

MACRO AND MICRO NUTRIENTS

PLANTS GET THEIR NOURISHMENT FROM MACRONUTRIENTS, WHICH ARE ABSORBED IN LARGE QUANTITIES, AND MICRO NUTRIENTS, WHICH ARE ABSORBED IN SMALL TO MINUTE QUANTITIES.

MACRO NUTRIENTS INCLUDE:

N	NITROGEN
P	PHOSPHORUS
K	POTASSIUM

MICRONUTRIENTS:

CA	CALCIUM
S	SULFUR
FE	IRON
MG	MAGNESIUM
B	BORON
MN	MANGANESE
ZN	ZINC
MO	MOLYBDENUM
CU	COPPER
CO	COBALT

DEFICIENCY AND TOXICITY OF THESE ELEMENTS AT MACRO AND MICRO LEVELS AFFECTS THE STATUS OF YOUR PLANTS AND CAN EVEN ALTER THE FLAVOR. I RECOMMEND LOOKING UP SPECIFICS ON THE INTERNET BECAUSE THE LITERATURE AVAILABLE IS RATHER VAST. BE AWARE THAT MOST OF THE NUTRIENTS SOLD TODAY PROVIDE ONLY MACRONUTRIENTS. HOWEVER, THERE ARE SEVERAL WAYS TO PROVIDE MICRONUTRIENTS. FOR THESE TECHNIQUES, I ALSO SUGGEST LOOKING UP SPECIFICS AND DOING A LITTLE RESEARCH OF YOUR OWN. THIS IS NOT THE FOCUS OF THIS MANUAL. ONLY A COUPLE OF EXAMPLES WILL FOLLOW.

ORGANIC FERTILIZERS

THERE ARE SEVERAL WAYS TO PRODUCE ORGANIC FERTILIZERS. HERE ARE TWO EXAMPLES:

COMPOST TEA

A

FILL THE BUCKET WITH WATER AND ADD SOME COMPOST. STIR.

Bucket

Compost

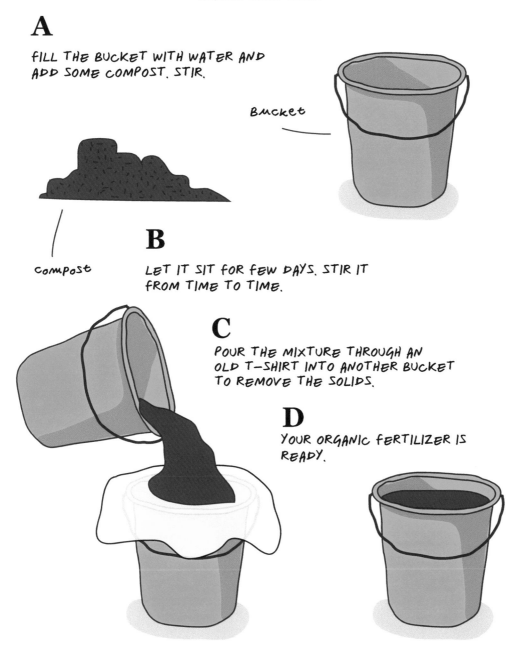

B

LET IT SIT FOR FEW DAYS. STIR IT FROM TIME TO TIME.

C

POUR THE MIXTURE THROUGH AN OLD T-SHIRT INTO ANOTHER BUCKET TO REMOVE THE SOLIDS.

D

YOUR ORGANIC FERTILIZER IS READY.

Human

URINE

YES, YOU READ THIS CORRECTLY. NORMALLY FOR THIS PRACTICE, FISH URINE IS USED. THE TECHNIQUE IS CALLED AQUAPONICS. IT IS A CLOSED LOOP: FISH FERTILIZE WATER FOR THE PLANTS AND PLANTS CLEAN THE WATER FOR THE FISH. THIS TECHNIQUE IS NORMALLY USED TO FARM BOTH FISH AND PLANTS AT THE SAME TIME. FROM A CHEMICAL POINT OF VIEW, FISH URINE IS IDENTICAL TO HUMAN URINE. OF COURSE IT NEEDS TO BE DILUTED, OTHERWISE IT WILL "BURN" THE PLANT. HERE IS A RECOMMENDATION FOUND ON WIKIPEDIA:

When diluted with water (at a 1:5 ratio for container-grown annual crops with fresh growing medium each season, [21] or a 1:8 for more general use [20]), it can be applied directly to soil as a fertilizer. The fertilization effect of urine has been found to be comparable to that of commercial fertilizers with an equivalent NPK rating. [22]

http://en.wikipedia.org/wiki/Urine#Agriculture

WHAT I REALLY LIKE ABOUT THIS CONCEPT IS THAT IT MAKES ME REALIZE THAT WE REALLY ARE WHAT WE EAT AND THAT WASTE IN NATURE DOES NOT EXIST.
THERE ARE MANY RESOURCES AVAILABLE ON THIS TOPIC. HERE ARE A FEW PAPERS I RECOMMEND YOU READ:

S. A. Esray, I. Anderson, A. Hillers, R. Sawyer, *Closing the Loop. Ecological Sanitation for Food Security.* Publications on Water Resources No. 18, Mexico 2001.

H. Jonsson, *Guidelines on the Use of Urine and Feces in Crop Production.* EcoSanRes Publications Series, Report 2004-2. Stockholm Environment Institute; Stockholm, Sweden. AVAILABLE FROM WWW.ECOSANRES.ORG.

R. Gensch, A. Miso, G. Itchon, *Urine as Liquid Fertilizer in Agricultural Production in the Philippines.* A Practical Field Guide, Xavier University Press, 2011.

AN AIR PUMP IS MADE OF THREE PARTS: THE PUMP ITSELF (NORMALLY IN THE WATER) A HOSE THAT DIRECTS THE AIR FROM THE PUMP, AND A "STONE" THAT KEEPS THE PIPE AT THE BOTTOM OF THE TANK AND RELEASES SMALL AIR BUBBLES.

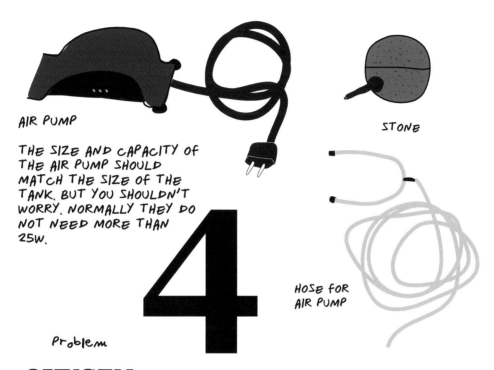

AIR PUMP

STONE

THE SIZE AND CAPACITY OF THE AIR PUMP SHOULD MATCH THE SIZE OF THE TANK. BUT YOU SHOULDN'T WORRY. NORMALLY THEY DO NOT NEED MORE THAN 25W.

HOSE FOR AIR PUMP

Problem

4

OXYGEN

OXYGEN CAN BE PROVIDED TO THE PLANTS IN DIFFERENT WAYS. MOST COMMONLY, HYDROPONIC SYSTEMS USE AIR PUMPS, JUST LIKE THE ONES USED FOR AQUARIUMS. FISH NEED OXYGEN TOO.

THERE ARE MANY DIFFERENT SYSTEMS TO GET OXYGEN TO THE ROOTS. I WILL NAME A FEW HERE: WITH THE FILM TECHNIQUE, ROOTS ABSORB NUTRIENTS FROM A THIN STREAM (A FILM) OF WATER; WITH AEROPONICS, THE WATER AND NUTRIENTS ARE VAPORIZED AND ABSORBED DIRECTLY BY THE ROOTS; AND WITH VERTICAL GARDENING SYSTEMS, THE PLANTS ARE NOURISHED BY DROPS FROM THE TOP AND THE EXCESS WATER IS COLLECTED AT THE BOTTOM AND SOMETIMES PUMPED BACK INTO A RESERVOIR ON TOP OF THE SYSTEM. IN THIS LAST SYSTEM, THE PLANTS ARE INSTALLED IN A PIPE WHICH CONTAINS A SPECIAL SPONGE OR EXPANDED CLAY TO KEEP THE PLANTS MOIST AND PROVIDE OXYGEN.

SOLUTION (A)
USE AN AIR PUMP

ELIOOO #8   plants

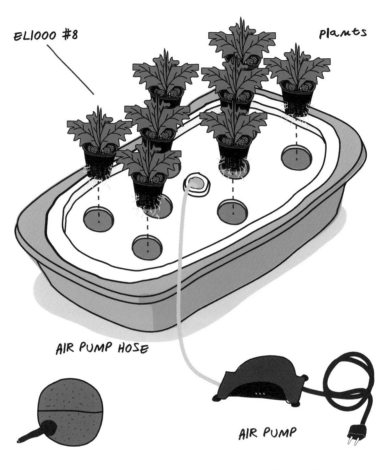

AIR PUMP HOSE

AIR PUMP

AIR PUMP STONE
IS ATTACHED TO
THE OTHER SIDE
OF THE AIR PUMP
AND HOSE.

THE AIR PUMP PROVIDES
OXYGEN TO THE WATER.
AS IT EVAPORATES, YOU
WILL NEED TO ADD WATER
AND FERTILIZER.

THIS DEVICE NEEDS ELECTRICITY.

SOLUTION (B)
DRIPPING SYSTEM

PLASTIC BOTTLE WITH FERTILIZER.
THE FERTILIZER IS DISPENSED WITH
A SIMPLE CORK SYSTEM, AND IS
RELEASED DROP BY DROP.

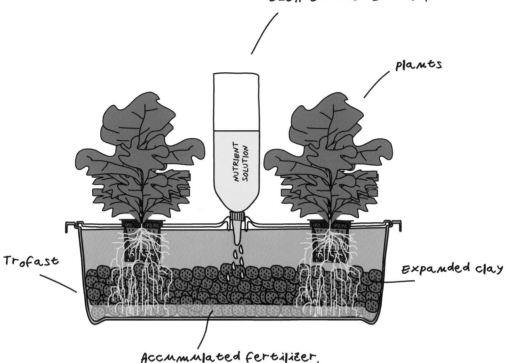

plants

Trofast

Expanded clay

NUTRIENT
SOLUTION

Accumulated fertilizer.

THE FERTILIZED WATER MUST BE RELEASED
LITTLE BY LITTLE, JUST ENOUGH TO KEEP THE EXPANDED
CLAY MOIST. THE ONLY PROBLEM WITH THIS SYSTEM IS THAT
THE CLAY MUST ALWAYS REMAIN MOIST. SO IF IT IS LEFT
IN THE SUN, IT MIGHT REQUIRE NUTRIENT SOLUTION
MORE OFTEN AS IT MAY EVAPORATE FASTER.

YOU ALSO HAVE TO MAKE SURE THAT THE RAIN
WATER DOES NOT LEAK IN, AS IT WILL DILUTE THE
NUTRIENT SOLUTION.

I RECOMMEND READING THIS:
R. Kourik, *Drip Irrigation for Every Landscape and All Climates*. Metamorphic Press, 2009.

SOLUTION (B1)

DRIPPING SYSTEM

THE WATER WITH NUTRIENTS IS STORED IN A BOTTLE OR RESERVOIR AND DRIPS DOWN INTO THE OTHER TRAYS.

FOR THE DRIPPING BOTTLE SYSTEM, YOU CAN USE A SIMPLE BOTTLE CAP WITH A HOLE OR A SPECIALLY DESIGNED CAP TO FIT THE BOTTLE.

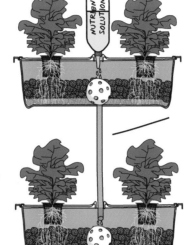

THE EXCESS WATER WITH NUTRIENTS GOES DOWN THE HOSE AND IS COLLECTED IN THE LOWER ONE.

YOU HAVE TO MAKE SURE THAT THE PIPE DOES NOT GET CLOGGED. A WELL-PLACED WHIFFLE BALL CAN DO THE TRICK

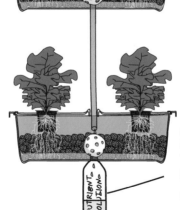

A THE END OF THE SYSTEM, PUT A RESERVOIR JUST LIKE THE ONE ON TOP. REPLACE THE BOTTLE WITH A SOLUTION OF FERTILIZER.

SOLUTION (C)
circulating Hydroponics

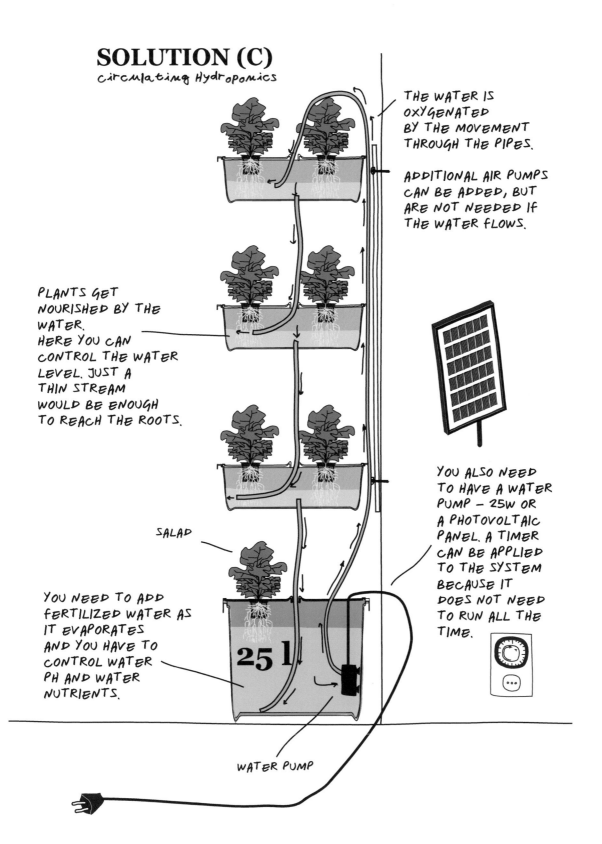

THE WATER IS OXYGENATED BY THE MOVEMENT THROUGH THE PIPES.

ADDITIONAL AIR PUMPS CAN BE ADDED, BUT ARE NOT NEEDED IF THE WATER FLOWS.

PLANTS GET NOURISHED BY THE WATER.
HERE YOU CAN CONTROL THE WATER LEVEL. JUST A THIN STREAM WOULD BE ENOUGH TO REACH THE ROOTS.

SALAD

YOU ALSO NEED TO HAVE A WATER PUMP – 25W OR A PHOTOVOLTAIC PANEL. A TIMER CAN BE APPLIED TO THE SYSTEM BECAUSE IT DOES NOT NEED TO RUN ALL THE TIME.

YOU NEED TO ADD FERTILIZED WATER AS IT EVAPORATES AND YOU HAVE TO CONTROL WATER PH AND WATER NUTRIENTS.

25 l

WATER PUMP

NUTRIENT CONCENTRATION AND PH

IN CIRCULATING SYSTEMS IT IS IMPORTANT TO MAINTAIN THE RIGHT
NUTRIENT CONCENTRATION AS IT WILL GET DILUTED OVER TIME AS
PLANTS GROW. NUTRIENT CONCENTRATION IS MEASURED VIA PPM OR
TDS — PART PER MILLION AND TOTAL DISSOLVED SOLIDS. THIS IS ALSO
COMMONLY REFERRED TO AS EC OR THE ELECTRICAL CONDUCTIVITY OF
A SOLUTION, AS THIS IS WHAT YOU ARE MEASURING.

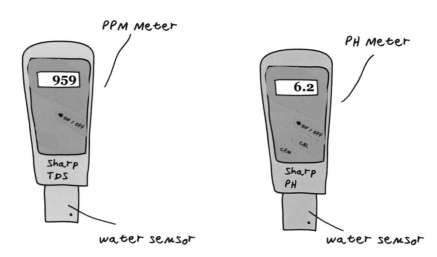

PPM Meter

959

Sharp
TDS

water sensor

PH Meter

6.2

Sharp
PH

water sensor

THE NUTRIENTS WILL NOT DO A PLANT ANY GOOD IF THEY CANNOT
BE EASILY ABSORBED. A MAJOR FACTOR IN THIS IS ACIDITY, OR PH
OF THE SOIL OR THE HYDROPONIC SOLUTION.
PH IS MEASURED ON A SCALE OF 0-14, REPRESENTING THE
CONCENTRATION OF HYDRONIUM IONS. IT IS GENERALLY USED TO
DETERMINE WHETHER A SOLUTION IS ACIDIC OR BASIC. PURE WATER
IS CONSIDERED NEUTRAL WITH A PH OF 7. FOR A HYDROPONIC
INSTALLATION, THE PH SHOULD BE MONITORED AND KEPT
BETWEEN 6.0 AND 6.5. TO CORRECT THE PH OF THE NUTRIENT
SOLUTION, YOU CAN USE A PH CORRECTOR, OR JUST CHANGE THE
WATER IN THE RESERVOIR EVERY TWO WEEKS.

REGARDING THESE TECHNICAL ASPECTS THE BEST, MOST INSPIRING,
CLEAR AND USEFUL BOOK I HAVE EVER READ IS:

K. Roberto, *How-to Hydroponics. The Complete Guide To Building And Operating Your Own Indoor And Outdoor Hydroponic Gardens.* The Future Garden Press, New York, 2005.

ALSO AVAILABLE AT WWW.HOWTOHYDROPONICS.COM

SOLUTION (D)
NON-CIRCULATING HYDROPONICS

WITH THE NON-CIRCULATING METHOD, THE PLANT WILL DEVELOP ANAEROBIC ROOTS WHICH WILL BE UNDER THE WATER AND AEROBIC ROOTS WHICH WILL BE SUSPENDED IN THE AIR. THE PLANT WILL ONLY TAKE THE AMOUNT OF OXYGEN NEEDED.
THIS SYSTEM DOES NOT REQUIRE ELECTRICITY TO OXYGENATE THE WATER AS THE PLANT WILL DEVELOP AEROBIC ROOTS. THIS CONCEPT IS PATENTED BY THE UNIVERSITY OF HAWAII.

U.S. Patents 5.385.589 and 5.533.299

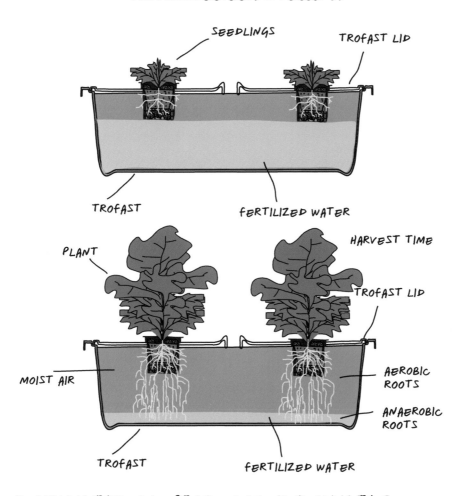

REGARDING THIS CONCEPT I RECOMMEND READING THESE:

B.A. Kratky, *Three Non-Circulating Hydroponic Methods For Growing Lettuce.*
T. M. Cadle, *The Secret of Non-Circulating Hydroponics. A Proven Method of Hydroponic Growing Without the High Cost.*
⤹ —— AVAILABLE ON ITUNES

NON CIRCULATING HYDROPONICS:
TIME AND SPACE

PLANTS NEED DIFFERENT AMOUNTS OF FERTILIZED WATER
TO GROW DEPENDING ON IF THEY ARE LEAFY VEGETABLES OR FRUIT
VEGETABLES. HERE IS AN EXAMPLE.

LETTUCE: 4 LITERS
TIME OF GROWTH: 30 DAYS

TOMATOES: 24-40 LITERS
LIFETIME: 1-2 YEARS (DEPENDING ON MANY FACTORS
INCLUDING THE TYPE OF PLANT)

CUCUMBER: 100 - 130 LITERS
TIME OF GROWTH: 80 DAYS

EL1000 CAPACITY

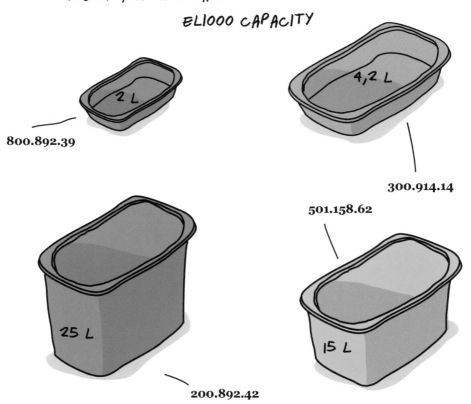

800.892.39

4,2 L

300.914.14

501.158.62

25 L

15 L

200.892.42

FOR PLANT REFERENCES SEE:
B.A. Kratky, 2004. *A Suspended Pot, Non-Circulating Hydroponic Method*.
Proceedings of the South Pacific Soilless Culture Conference, Acta Hort. 648. p. 83-89
IF YOU GOOGLE THIS YOU WILL BE ABLE TO FIND IT ON THE NET.

SOLUTION (D1)
Non-circulating Refill system

A SYSTEM THAT I HAVE BEEN EXPERIMENTING WITH IS SOMETHING I
CALL THE NON-CIRCULATING REFILL SYSTEM. THE IDEA IS SIMPLY TO LET
AEROBIC AND ANAEROBIC ROOTS DEVELOP. ALL YOU NEED TO DO IS REFILL
THE CONTAINER WITH FERTILIZED WATER TO KEEP THE WATER LEVEL
STEADY.
IN THIS WAY, THE PLANT WILL DEVELOP THE NECESSARY AEROBIC ROOTS
AND IT WILL KEEP GROWING. IT ONLY NEEDS A LITTLE WATER AT A TIME
— ONE LITER MAX IN THIS SYSTEM. PLEASE NOTE THAT THE PLANTS
MUST BE OF THE SAME STAGE OF DEVELOPMENT TO ENSURE THAT THE
SYSTEM IS RUNNING SMOOTHLY.

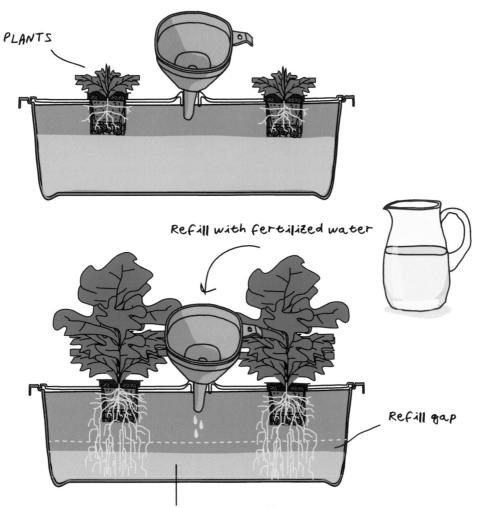

PLANTS

Refill with fertilized water

Refill gap

Keep fertilized water level "steady" so that plants can develop
aerobic roots to gather oxygen.

FIAT LUX

Problem

5

LIGHT

PLANT GROWTH IS DIRECTLY AFFECTED BY THE COLOR, INTENSITY, AND DURATION OF THE LIGHT THAT IT RECEIVES. IDEALLY, PLANTS SHOULD RECEIVE ABOUT 8 HOURS OF SUNLIGHT A DAY. ALTERNATIVELY YOU CAN USE FLUORESCENT "GROW" LIGHTS DESIGNED TO GROW PLANTS INDOORS. THIS WORKS FINE FOR LOW-LIGHT PLANTS SUCH AS HERBS OR LEAFY VEGETABLES. OTHERWISE, YOU CAN USE HIGH INTENSITY DISCHARGE LIGHTS ALSO KNOWN AS H.I.D. LIGHTS. LED LIGHTS ARE ALSO GETTING POPULAR. I HAVE TRIED A FEW BUT WITH LITTLE OR NO SUCCESS. THE TECHNOLOGY STILL NEEDS TO BE PROPERLY DEVELOPED I THINK.

FLUORESCENT GROW LIGHTS

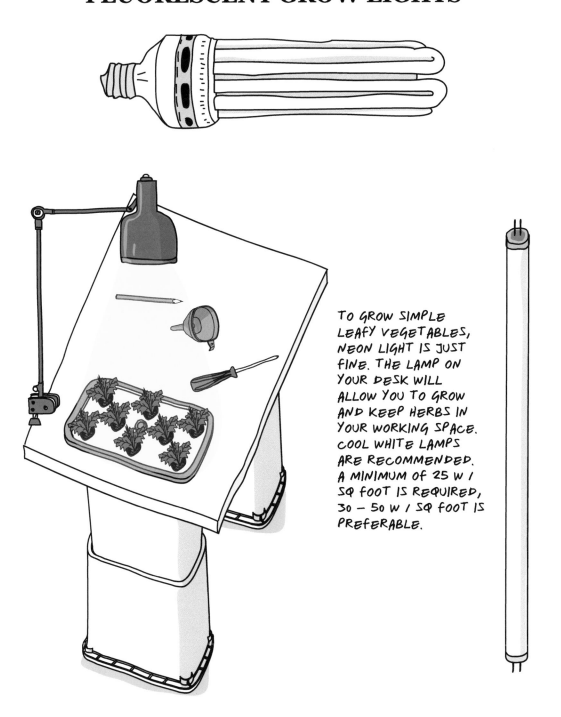

TO GROW SIMPLE LEAFY VEGETABLES, NEON LIGHT IS JUST FINE. THE LAMP ON YOUR DESK WILL ALLOW YOU TO GROW AND KEEP HERBS IN YOUR WORKING SPACE. COOL WHITE LAMPS ARE RECOMMENDED. A MINIMUM OF 25 W / SQ FOOT IS REQUIRED, 30 — 50 W / SQ FOOT IS PREFERABLE.

High Intensity Discharge
H.I.D. LIGHTING

IF YOU WANT TO ACHIEVE THE ULTIMATE GROWTH
POTENTIAL INDOORS, YOU WILL NEED TO USE H.I.D. LIGHTS.
THEY ARE DESIGNED TO PROVIDE THE MAXIMUM OUTPUT
OF PHOTOSYNTHETICALLY ACTIVE RADIATION (PAR) FOR
THE AMOUNT OF POWER CONSUMED.

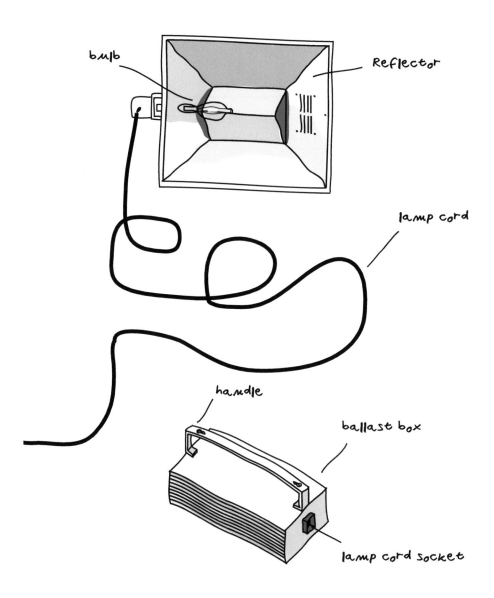

bulb

Reflector

lamp cord

handle

ballast box

lamp cord socket

H.I.D. BULBS

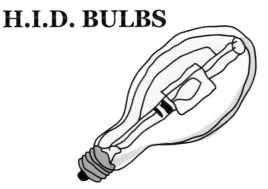

A METAL HALIDE — MH— LAMPS EMIT PRIMARILY BLUE LIGHT, MAKING THEM IDEAL FOR THE INITIAL GROWTH STAGE. MH BULBS WILL LAST FOR TWO YEARS, BUT IT IS SUGGESTED THAT YOU CHANGE THEM EVERY 12—14 MONTHS.

B HIGH PRESSURE SODIUM — HPS — LAMPS EMIT PRIMARILY RED LIGHT WHICH CAUSES INCREASED FLOWERING AND FRUITING DURING THE PLANT REPRODUCTIVE STAGE. HPS BULBS WILL LAST UP TO FIVE YEARS, BUT YOU SHOULD CHANGE THEM EVERY TWO. HID BULBS STILL WORK, BUT THEY GRADUALLY LOSE THEIR SPECTRUM (AND EFFECTIVENESS).

ADVICE:

GET A LAMP THAT WILL ACCEPT "CONVERSION" BULBS. USE YOUR MH BULB DURING THE INITIAL GROWTH STAGE, AND SWITCH TO THE HPS BULB AFTER THE FLOWERS APPEAR. MOST PLANTS GROW BEST WHEN EXPOSED TO 16—18 HRS OF LIGHT. GET A TIMER TO SET IT UP AUTOMATICALLY.

GROW AREA DIMENSION	LIGHT BULB POWER	DISTANCE FROM THE PLANTS

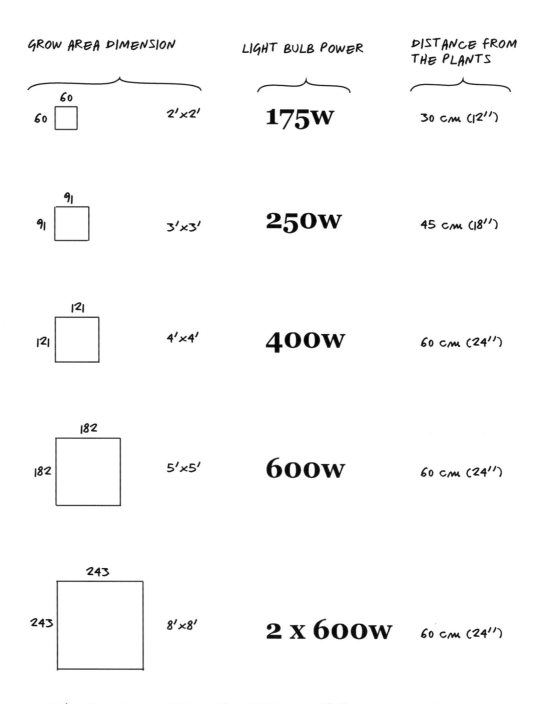

60 / 60 — 2'x2'	**175W**	30 cm (12'')
91 / 91 — 3'x3'	**250W**	45 cm (18'')
121 / 121 — 4'x4'	**400W**	60 cm (24'')
182 / 182 — 5'x5'	**600W**	60 cm (24'')
243 / 243 — 8'x8'	**2 x 600W**	60 cm (24'')

IF YOU RUN A 400 WATT LAMP 18 HRS PER DAY, YOU WILL USE 7.2 KWH. CHECK THE COST PER KWH ON YOUR ELECTRIC BILL AND MULTIPLY x 7.2 TO GET THE OPERATING COST. THIS SHOULD BE FROM 7-20 USD PER MONTH.

I RECOMMEND LOOKING IT UP AT: WWW.HYDROPONICS-SIMPLIFIED.COM

ELIOOO

GROW YOUR FOOD

ELIOOO #4

ELIOOO #4 IS IDEAL FOR GROWING HERBS IN THE KITCHEN.
IT IS SMALL AND COMPACT (20,5 X 29,7 X 10 CM) AND
YOU CAN GROW UP TO FOUR PLANTS, DEPENDING ON THEIR
SIZES.
KEEP IT NEXT TO A SUNNY WINDOW OR, A NORMAL NEON
LIGHT WOULD KEEP THE PLANT GROWING. ELIOOO #4 DOES
NOT REQUIRE ELECTRICITY.

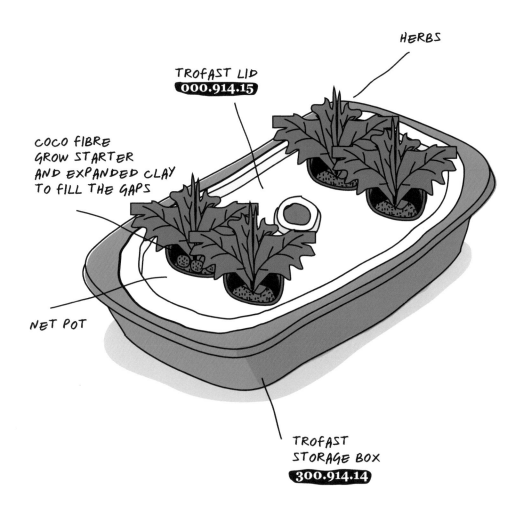

HERBS

TROFAST LID
000.914.15

COCO FIBRE
GROW STARTER
AND EXPANDED CLAY
TO FILL THE GAPS

NET POT

TROFAST
STORAGE BOX
300.914.14

ELIOOO #4:
WHAT YOU NEED

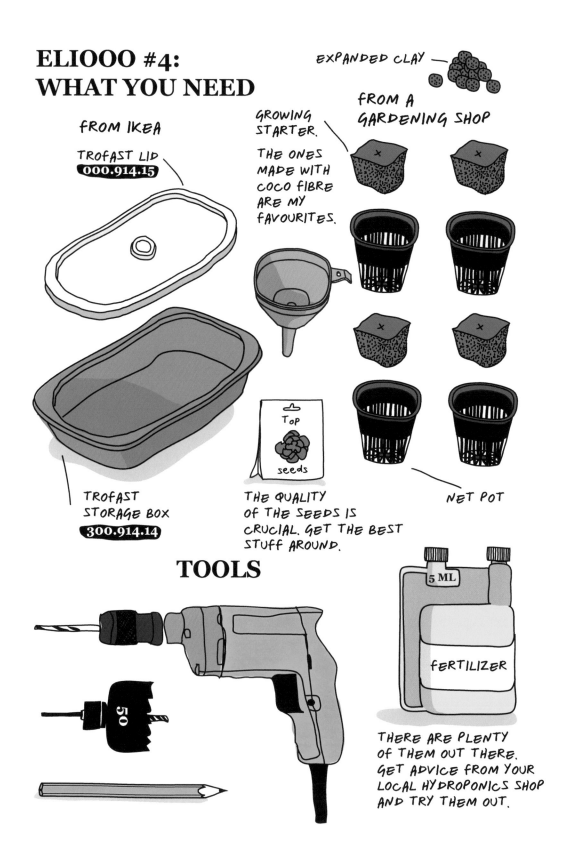

EXPANDED CLAY

FROM IKEA

GROWING STARTER.

FROM A GARDENING SHOP

TROFAST LID
000.914.15

THE ONES MADE WITH COCO FIBRE ARE MY FAVOURITES.

TROFAST STORAGE BOX
300.914.14

Top seeds

THE QUALITY OF THE SEEDS IS CRUCIAL. GET THE BEST STUFF AROUND.

NET POT

TOOLS

5 ML

FERTILIZER

THERE ARE PLENTY OF THEM OUT THERE. GET ADVICE FROM YOUR LOCAL HYDROPONICS SHOP AND TRY THEM OUT.

1 PREPARING THE GROW TRAYS

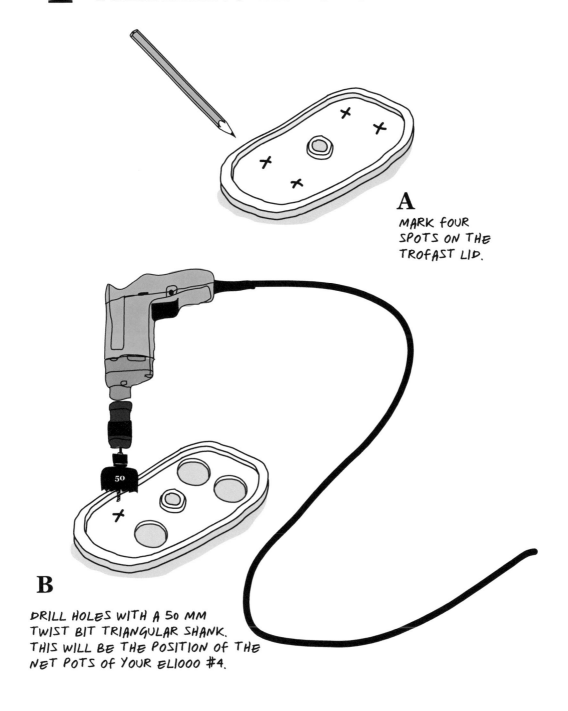

A

MARK FOUR
SPOTS ON THE
TROFAST LID.

B

DRILL HOLES WITH A 50 MM
TWIST BIT TRIANGULAR SHANK.
THIS WILL BE THE POSITION OF THE
NET POTS OF YOUR ELI000 #4.

2 INSTALLING THE NET POTS

A FILL THE TROFAST BOX WITH THE RIGHT SOLUTION OF WATER + FERTILIZER — SEE THE INSTRUCTIONS ON YOUR SEEDS. PLEASE NOTE THAT THE WATER LEVEL WILL HAVE TO ALMOST TOUCH THE ROOTS OF THE SEEDLINGS. IT SHOULD REQUIRE ABOUT 2 LITERS OF WATER.

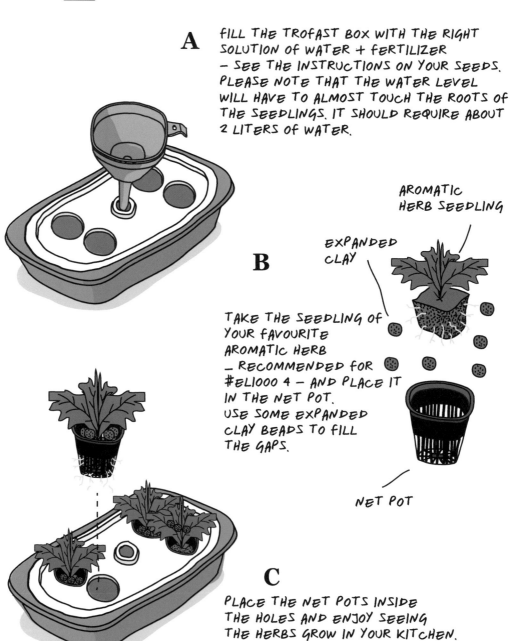

AROMATIC HERB SEEDLING

EXPANDED CLAY

B

TAKE THE SEEDLING OF YOUR FAVOURITE AROMATIC HERB — RECOMMENDED FOR #ELI000 4 — AND PLACE IT IN THE NET POT. USE SOME EXPANDED CLAY BEADS TO FILL THE GAPS.

NET POT

C

PLACE THE NET POTS INSIDE THE HOLES AND ENJOY SEEING THE HERBS GROW IN YOUR KITCHEN.

3 HARVESTING TIME

A AFTER TRANSPLANTING THE SEEDLINGS, THE ROOTS WILL GROW PARTLY IN THE AIR AND PARTLY IN THE WATER, SELF-REGULATING THE AMOUNT OF AIR THEY NEED TO GROW.

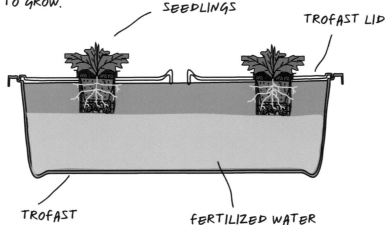

SEEDLINGS

TROFAST LID

TROFAST

FERTILIZED WATER

B THE PLANTS WILL DRINK ALL THE WATER. WHEN THE WATER IS FINISHED, IT WILL BE TIME TO HARVEST. I RECOMMEND CLONING THE PLANTS BEFORE THE FINAL HARVEST SO THAT YOU WILL BE ABLE TO REPLACE THEM IMMEDIATELY.

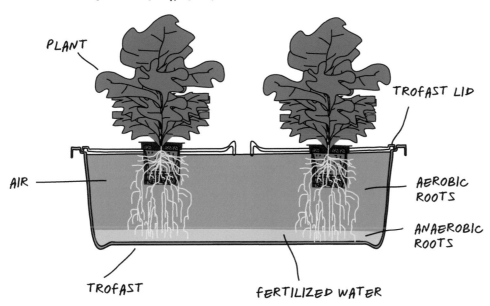

PLANT

TROFAST LID

AIR

AEROBIC ROOTS

ANAEROBIC ROOTS

TROFAST

FERTILIZED WATER

C

YOU CAN ALSO REFILL THE FERTILIZED WATER
LITTLE BY LITTLE. JUST KEEP ENOUGH SPACE
FOR THE AIR. THE PLANTS WILL DEVELOP THEIR OWN
AEROBIC ROOTS SO IT IS IMPORTANT THAT THE
AMOUNT OF WATER ADDED IS MINIMAL.

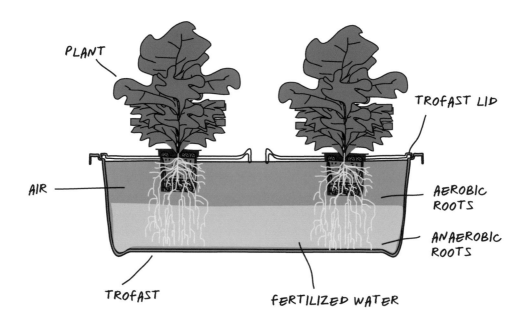

PLANT

TROFAST LID

AIR

AEROBIC
ROOTS

ANAEROBIC
ROOTS

TROFAST

FERTILIZED WATER

IN THIS MODEL, THE PLANTS NEED TO BE "WATERED"
MORE OFTEN. THE OTHER SYSTEMS DON'T NEED TO BE
WATERED AT ALL. THE PLANT WILL GROW AND IT WILL
ADAPT TO THE AMOUNT OF WATER AND AIR AVAILABLE.

4 ELIOOO #4 WALL INSTALLATION

#ELIOOO 4 CAN BE INSTALLED TO CREATE VERTICAL WALL
GARDENS WITH THE SIMPLE USE OF WALL ANCHORS.

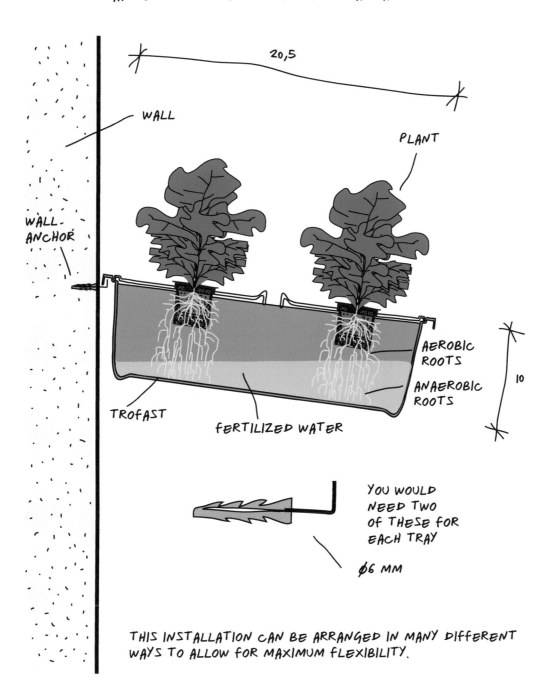

WALL

20,5

PLANT

WALL-
ANCHOR

AEROBIC
ROOTS

ANAEROBIC
ROOTS

10

TROFAST

FERTILIZED WATER

YOU WOULD
NEED TWO
OF THESE FOR
EACH TRAY

Ø6 MM

THIS INSTALLATION CAN BE ARRANGED IN MANY DIFFERENT
WAYS TO ALLOW FOR MAXIMUM FLEXIBILITY.

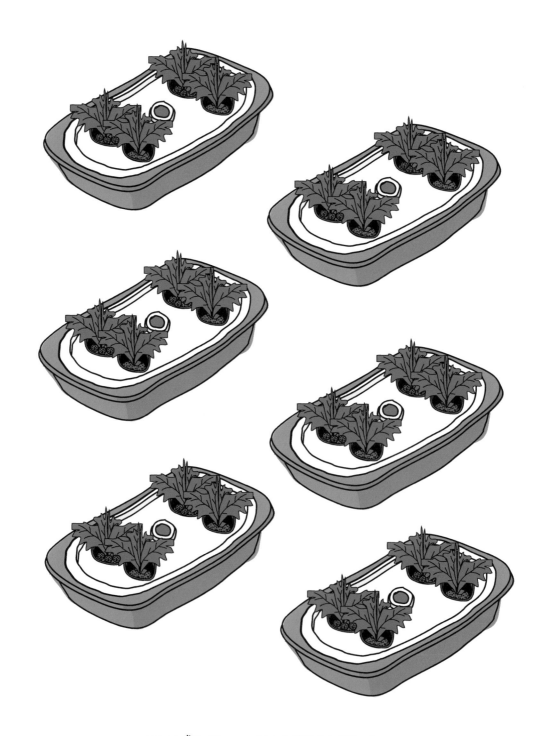

ELIOOO #4 FREE WALL INSTALLATION

ELIOOO #8

ELIOOO #8 IS A SIMPLE MODEL IDEAL
FOR GROWING HERBS IN THE KITCHEN,
OFFICE, OR WHEREVER YOU WANT.
KEEP IT NEXT TO A SUNNY WINDOW, OR
A NORMAL NEON LIGHT. ELIOOO #8 CAN
ALSO BE HUNG ON THE WALL TO CREATE
A VERTICAL GARDEN SYSTEM.

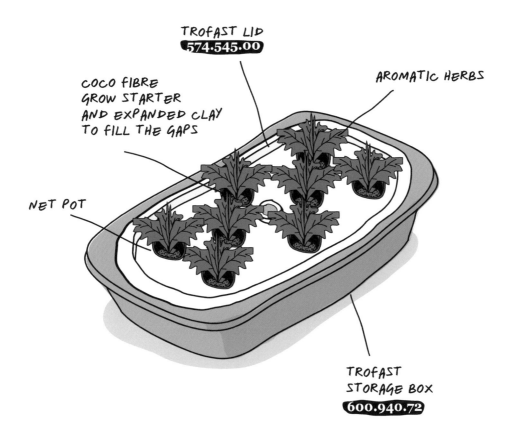

TROFAST LID
574.545.00

COCO FIBRE
GROW STARTER
AND EXPANDED CLAY
TO FILL THE GAPS

AROMATIC HERBS

NET POT

TROFAST
STORAGE BOX
600.940.72

ELIOOO #8: WHAT YOU NEED

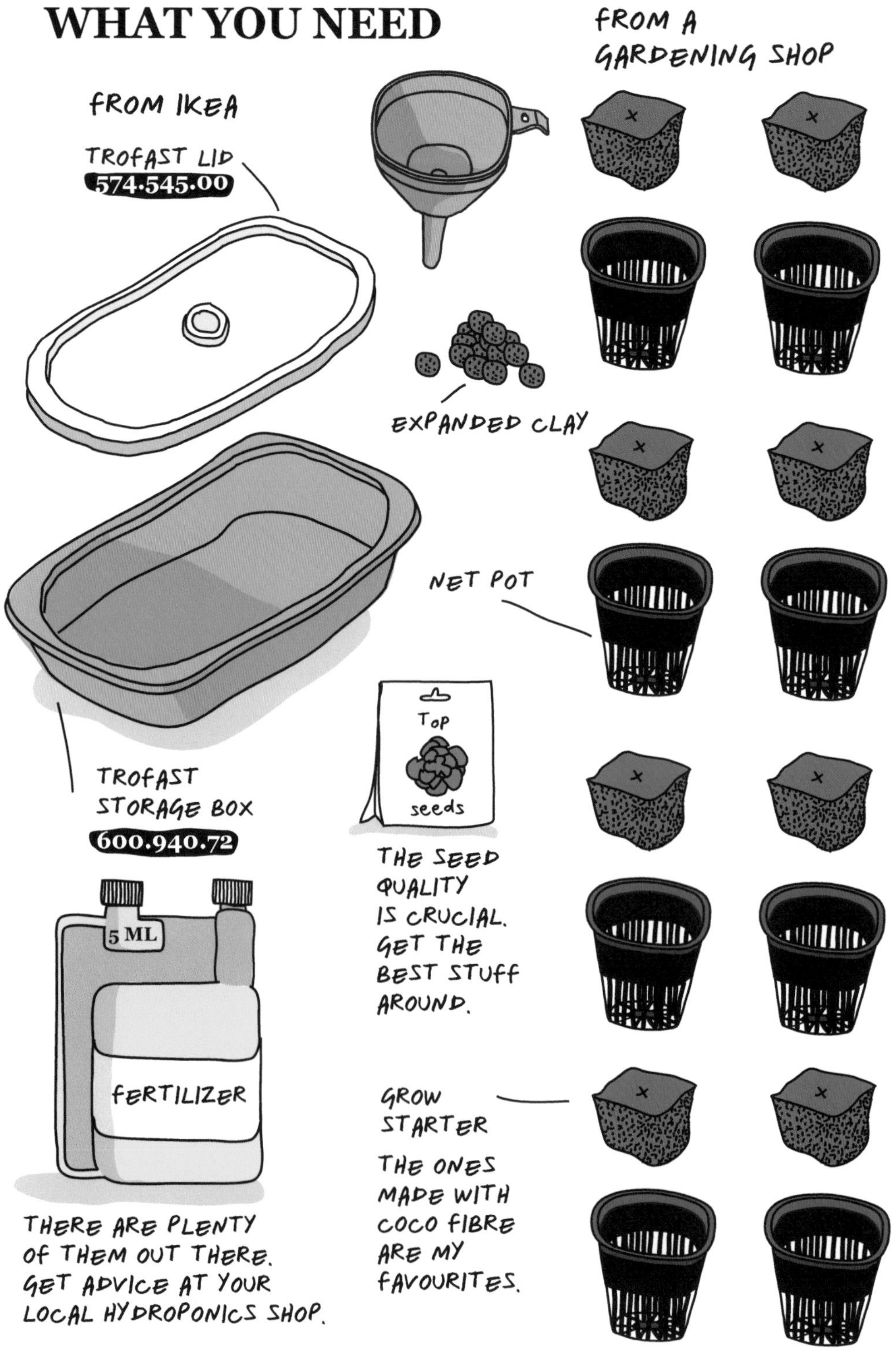

FROM IKEA

TROFAST LID
574.545.00

FROM A GARDENING SHOP

EXPANDED CLAY

NET POT

TROFAST STORAGE BOX
600.940.72

5 ML

FERTILIZER

THERE ARE PLENTY OF THEM OUT THERE. GET ADVICE AT YOUR LOCAL HYDROPONICS SHOP.

Top seeds

THE SEED QUALITY IS CRUCIAL. GET THE BEST STUFF AROUND.

GROW STARTER

THE ONES MADE WITH COCO FIBRE ARE MY FAVOURITES.

TOOLS

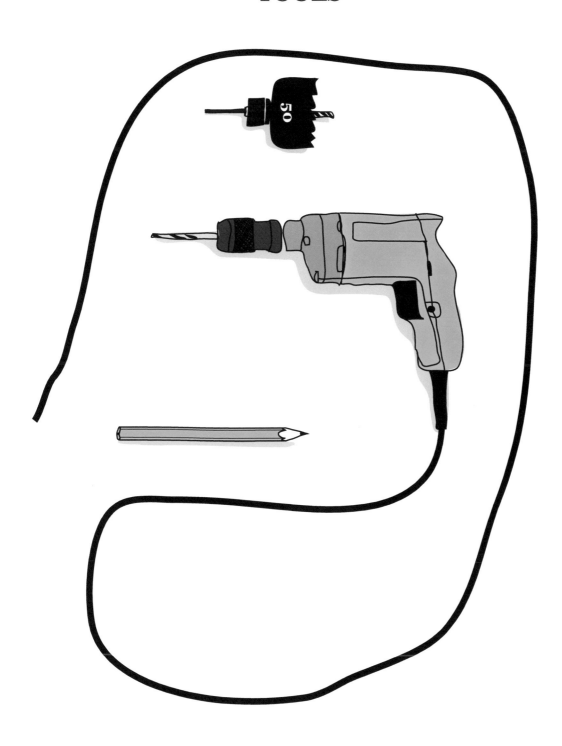

1 PREPARING THE GROW TRAYS

A

MARK EIGHT SPOTS ON THE
TROFAST LID WITH A PENCIL.

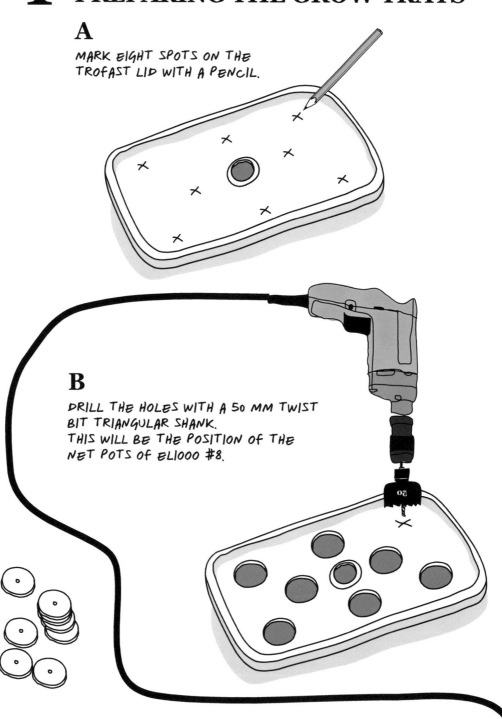

B

DRILL THE HOLES WITH A 50 MM TWIST
BIT TRIANGULAR SHANK.
THIS WILL BE THE POSITION OF THE
NET POTS OF EL1000 #8.

2 INSTALLING THE NET POTS

A

FILL THE TROFAST BOX WITH THE RIGHT
SOLUTION OF WATER + FERTILIZER. PLEASE
NOTE THAT THE WATER LEVEL WILL HAVE TO
ALMOST TOUCH THE ROOTS OF THE SEEDLINGS.
ELI000 #8 WILL CONTAIN APPROXIMATELY
4,2 LITERS OF WATER. MEASURE IT
BECAUSE THE ACTUAL AMOUNT DEPENDS
ON THE TYPE OF NET POT YOU ARE USING.

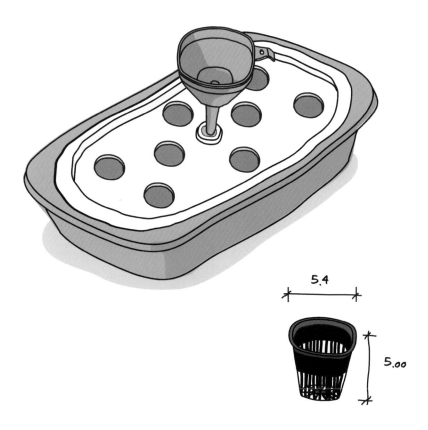

5.4

5.00

B

TAKE THE SEEDLING AND PLACE IT IN THE NET POT. USE SOME EXPANDED CLAY BEADS TO FILL THE GAPS.

AROMATIC HERB SEEDLING

EXPANDED CLAY

NET POT

C

PLACE THE NET POTS INSIDE THE HOLES AND ENJOY SEEING YOUR FAVOURITE AROMATIC HERBS GROW.

3 ELIOOO #8 WALL INSTALLATION

#ELIOOO 8 CAN BE INSTALLED TO CREATE VERTICAL WALL
GARDENS WITH THE SIMPLE USE OF WALL ANCHORS
AND PING PONG BALLS.

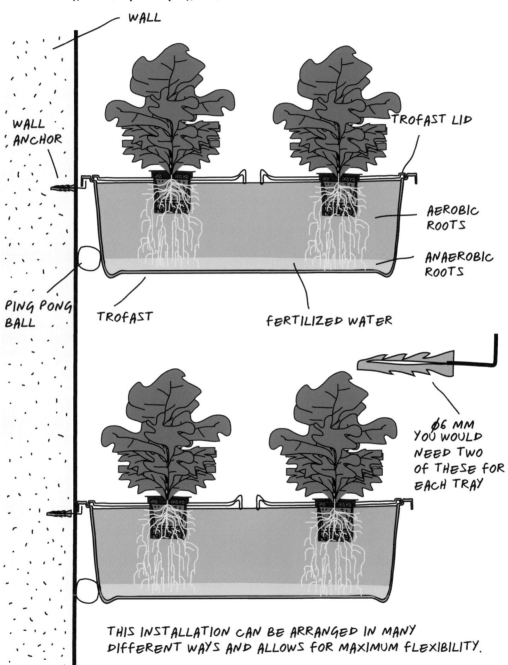

WALL

WALL
ANCHOR

TROFAST LID

AEROBIC
ROOTS

ANAEROBIC
ROOTS

PING PONG
BALL

TROFAST

FERTILIZED WATER

Ø6 MM
YOU WOULD
NEED TWO
OF THESE FOR
EACH TRAY

THIS INSTALLATION CAN BE ARRANGED IN MANY
DIFFERENT WAYS AND ALLOWS FOR MAXIMUM FLEXIBILITY.

HOW TO PROCEED

A MARK TWO SPOTS ON THE WALL WITH A DISTANCE OF 23 CM APART.

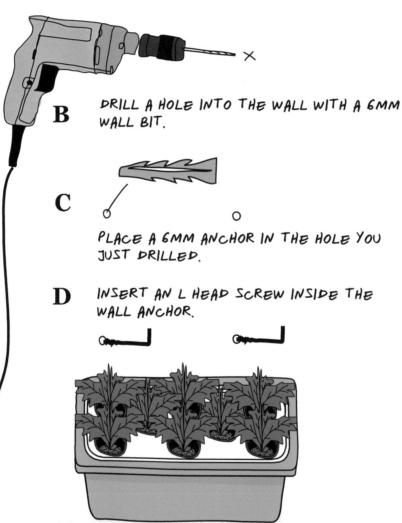

B DRILL A HOLE INTO THE WALL WITH A 6MM WALL BIT.

C PLACE A 6MM ANCHOR IN THE HOLE YOU JUST DRILLED.

D INSERT AN L HEAD SCREW INSIDE THE WALL ANCHOR.

E HANG THE ELI000 #8 ON THE WALL AND REPEAT TO CREATE A VERTICAL GARDEN FACADE.

IF YOU WANT TO KEEP IT
STRAIGHT, PLACE A
PING PONG BALL BETWEEN
THE WALL AND THE BOX.

OTHERWISE JUST LEAN IT
AGAINST THE WALL AS SHOWN
WITH ELI000 #4

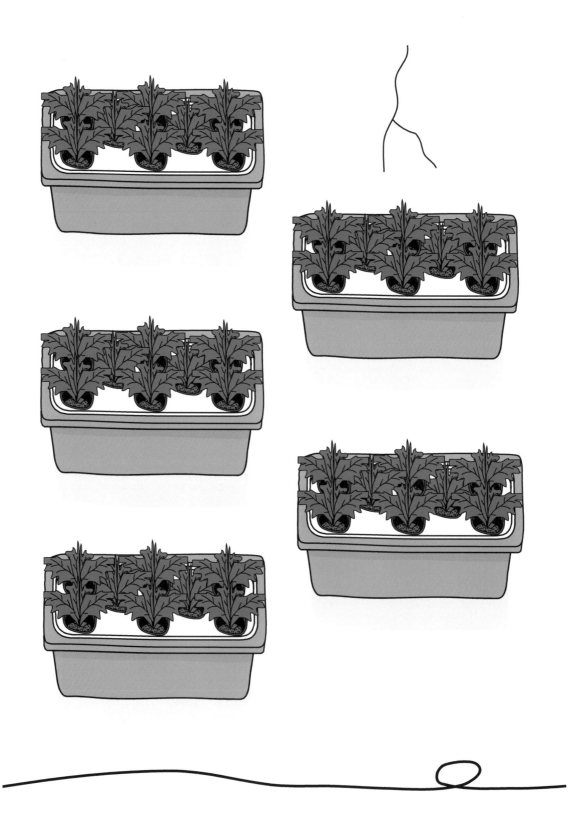

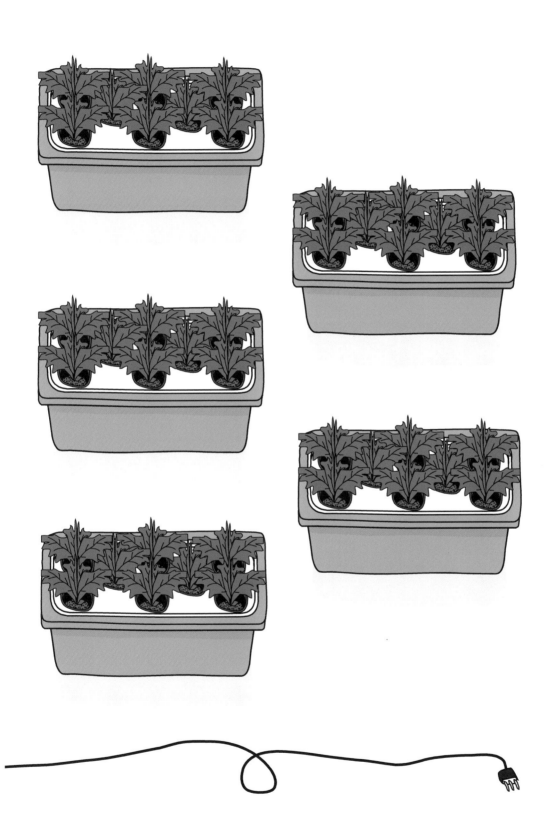

ELIOOO #DESK

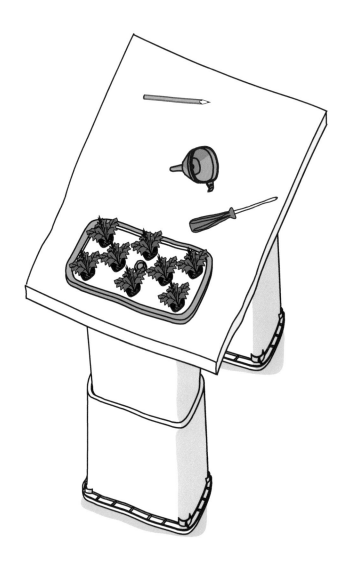

ELIOOO DESK IS ABLE TO HOLD UP TO EIGHT POTS. IT IS IDEAL
FOR GROWING AROMATIC HERBS AND LEAFY VEGETABLES IN YOUR
WORKPLACE. THE DESK IS MADE OF A COMBINATION OF LARGE
RESERVOIRS THAT ARE SUSPENDED IN THE TABLE TOP, WHICH IS
DESIGNED TO FIT ELIOOO #8. THE BOTTOM OF ONE RESERVOIR
CAN BE USED TO STORE GARDENING TOOLS.

ELIOOO DESK. WHAT YOU NEED

FROM IKEA:

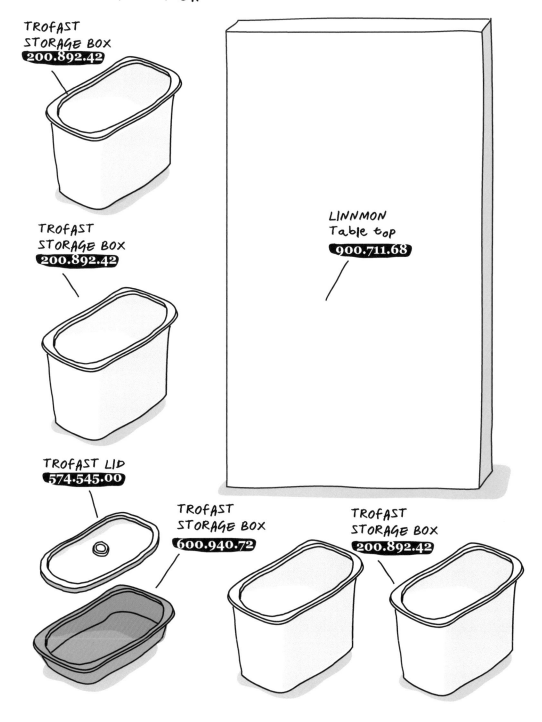

TROFAST
STORAGE BOX
200.892.42

TROFAST
STORAGE BOX
200.892.42

TROFAST LID
574.545.00

LINNMON
Table top
900.711.68

TROFAST
STORAGE BOX
600.940.72

TROFAST
STORAGE BOX
200.892.42

FROM A GARDENING SHOP

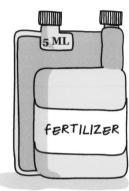

THERE ARE PLENTY
OF THEM OUT THERE.
GET ADVICE AT YOUR
LOCAL HYDROPONICS SHOP.

EXPANDED CLAY

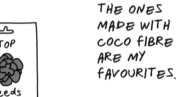

GROWING
STARTER

THE ONES
MADE WITH
COCO FIBRE
ARE MY
FAVOURITES.

THE SEED
QUALITY
IS CRUCIAL.
GET THE
BEST STUFF
AROUND.

TOP
seeds

NET POT

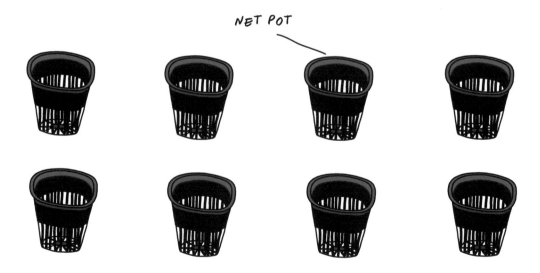

TOOLS

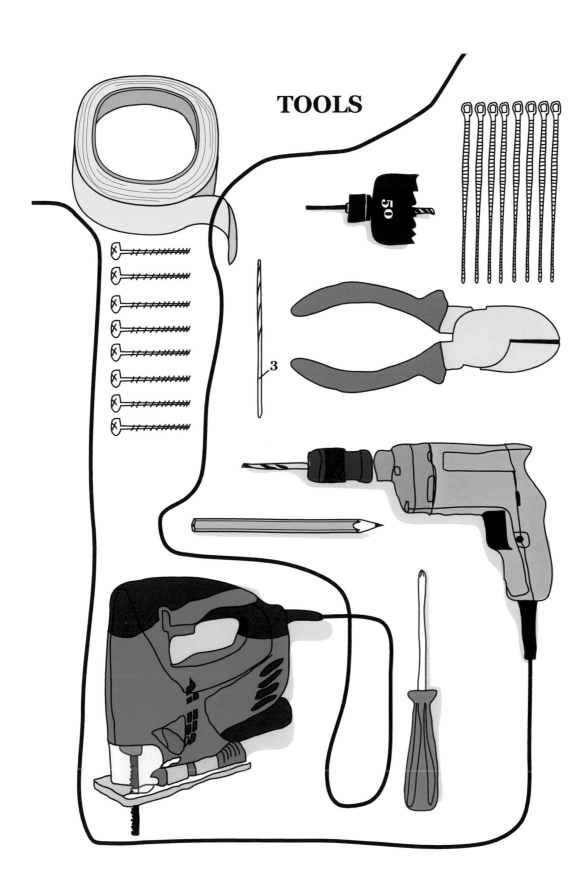

50

3

1 PREPARING THE TABLE TOP

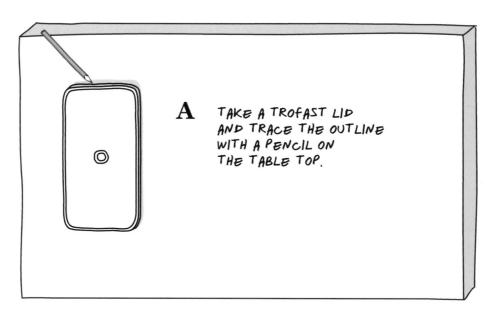

A TAKE A TROFAST LID AND TRACE THE OUTLINE WITH A PENCIL ON THE TABLE TOP.

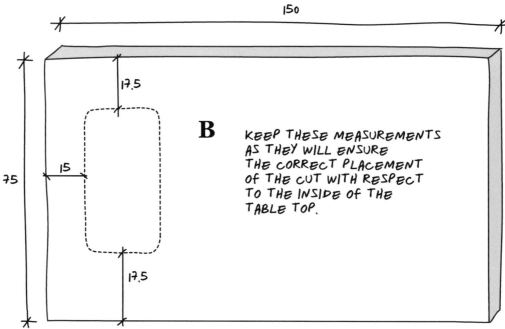

B KEEP THESE MEASUREMENTS AS THEY WILL ENSURE THE CORRECT PLACEMENT OF THE CUT WITH RESPECT TO THE INSIDE OF THE TABLE TOP.

C CORRECT THE FOUR CORNERS WITH A PENCIL AND MAKE THEM A BIT MORE "SHARP." THIS IS IMPORTANT SO THAT THE TROFAST BOX CAN FIT INSIDE THE TABLE TOP. IF THE CORNER IS NOT GOOD ENOUGH, YOU WILL NOTICE IT. BUT NO WORRIES, YOU WILL BE ABLE TO CORRECT IT AFTERWARDS. THE CUT EDGE SHOULD BE HIDDEN UNDER THE BOX.

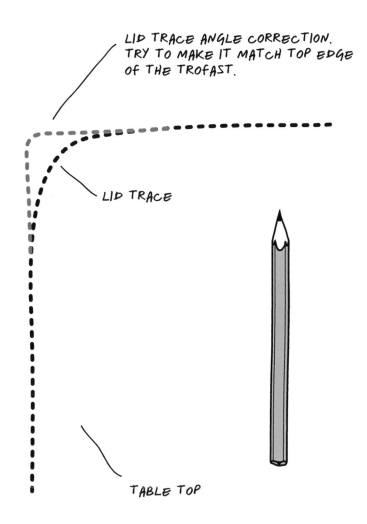

LID TRACE ANGLE CORRECTION. TRY TO MAKE IT MATCH TOP EDGE OF THE TROFAST.

LID TRACE

TABLE TOP

D TAKE A DRILL AND MAKE A HOLE
USING A 50 MM TWIST BIT TRIANGULAR
SHANK. THIS WILL ALLOW YOU TO START
CUTTING WITH A JIGSAW.

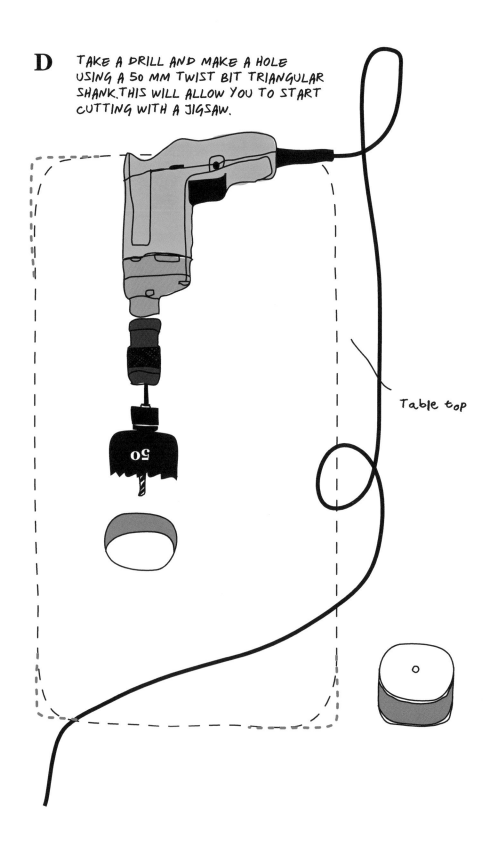

Table top

E PLUG IN THE JIGSAW AND START CUTTING ALONG THE LINE YOU HAVE DRAWN. TAKE YOUR TIME, THERE IS NO RUSH AND PLEASE BE CAREFUL BECAUSE JIGSAWS ARE DANGEROUS TOOLS.

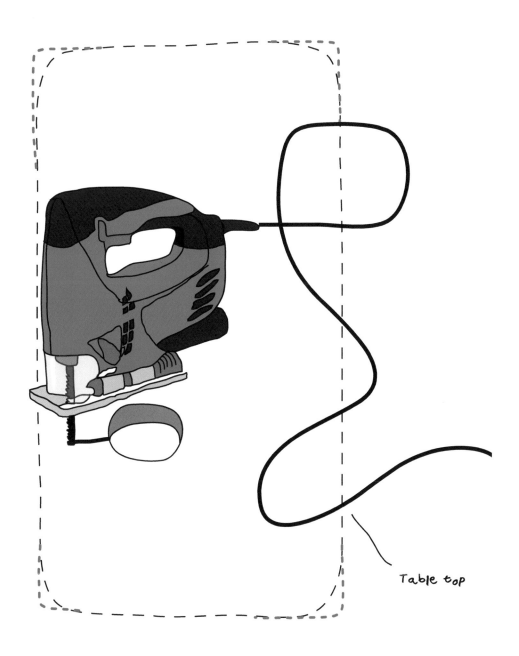

Table top

F   CONGRATULATIONS!
THE CUT IS DONE. SIT BACK AND ENJOY THE GOOD WORK

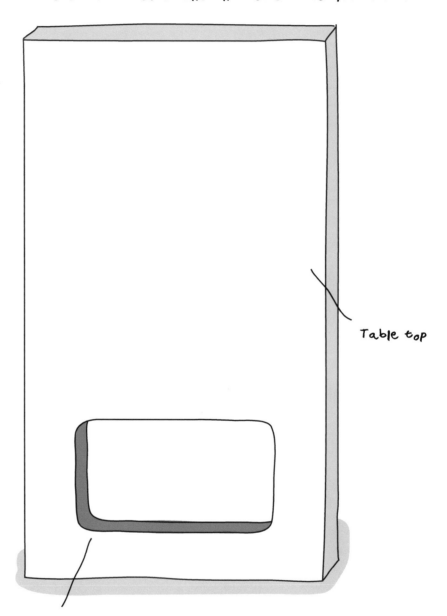

Table top

THIS CUT MIGHT BE A LITTLE ROUGH.
NO WORRIES, NOBODY WILL SEE IT.

2 PREPARING THE SUPPORTS

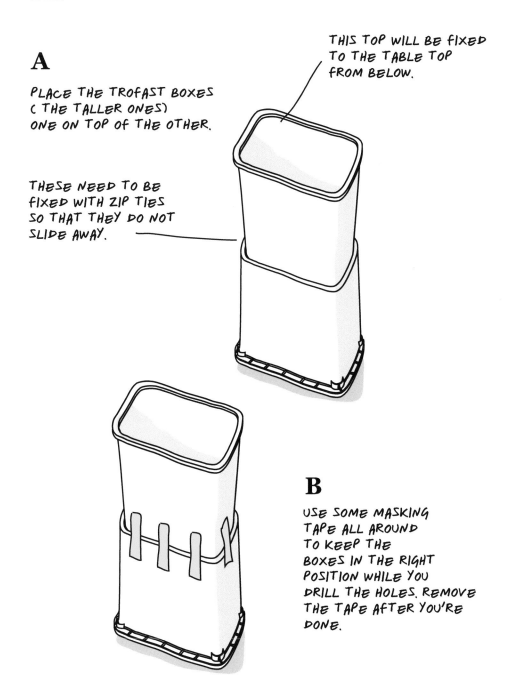

A

PLACE THE TROFAST BOXES
(THE TALLER ONES)
ONE ON TOP OF THE OTHER.

THESE NEED TO BE
FIXED WITH ZIP TIES
SO THAT THEY DO NOT
SLIDE AWAY.

THIS TOP WILL BE FIXED
TO THE TABLE TOP
FROM BELOW.

B

USE SOME MASKING
TAPE ALL AROUND
TO KEEP THE
BOXES IN THE RIGHT
POSITION WHILE YOU
DRILL THE HOLES. REMOVE
THE TAPE AFTER YOU'RE
DONE.

C PLACE THEM ON TOP EACH THE OTHER AND MARK THREE SETS OF POINTS AS SHOWN HERE.

D KEEP THE BOXES FIXED AND DRILL HOLES ON THE POINTS YOU HAVE MARKED. YOU HAVE TO DRILL BOTH BOXES, SO MAKE SURE THEY DO NOT MOVE WHILE YOU DRILL. HOLES MUST MATCH UP.

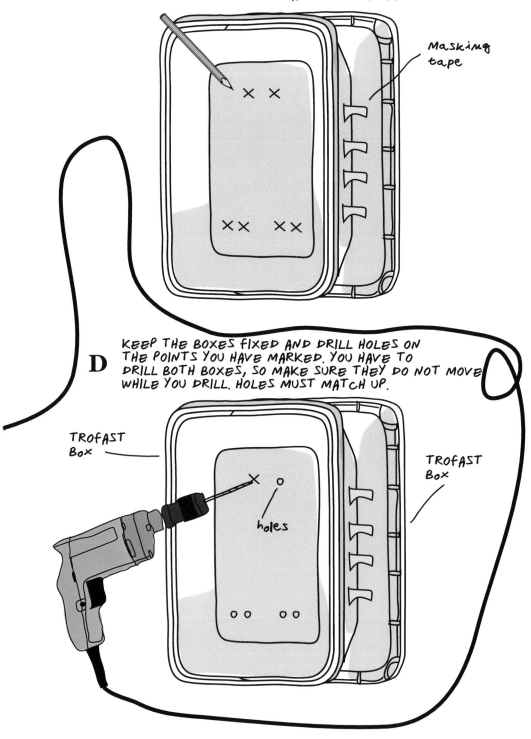

Masking tape

TROFAST Box

TROFAST Box

holes

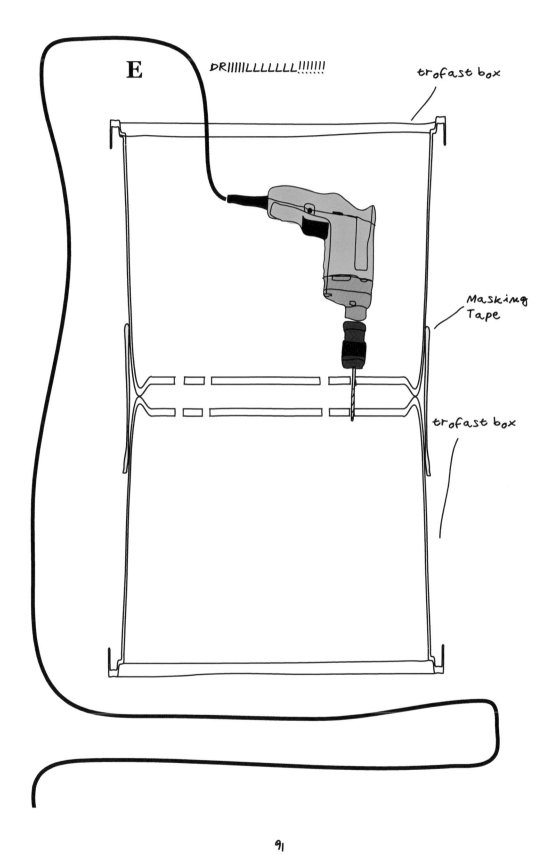

E   DRIIIIILLLLLLL!!!!!!!

trofast box

Masking Tape

trofast box

F SECURE THE BOXES BY PASSING A ZIP TIE THROUGH THE HOLES AND PULLING IT TIGHT. THIS PROCESS IS A BIT TEDIOUS BUT IT WORKS. BE PATIENT.

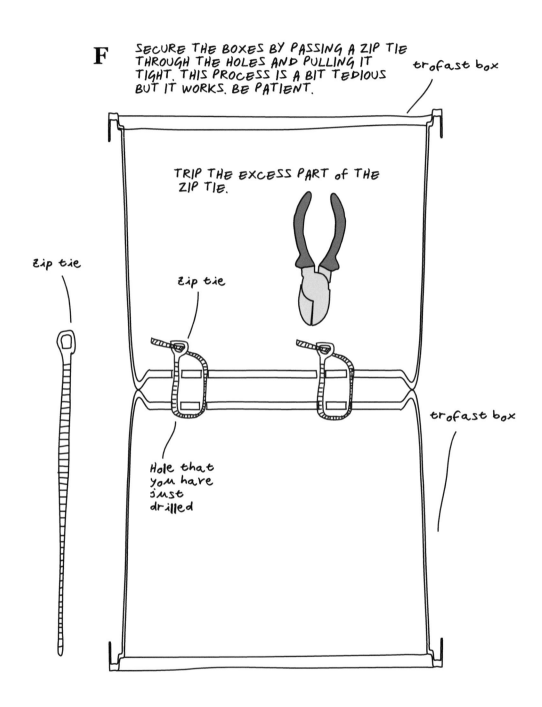

trofast box

TRIP THE EXCESS PART of THE ZIP TIE.

zip tie

zip tie

Hole that you have just drilled

trofast box

F DO THE SAME WITH THE OTHER PAIR OF BOXES.

3 FIXING THE TABLE TOP
NOW IT'S TIME TO FIX THE TOP TO THE SUPPORTS.

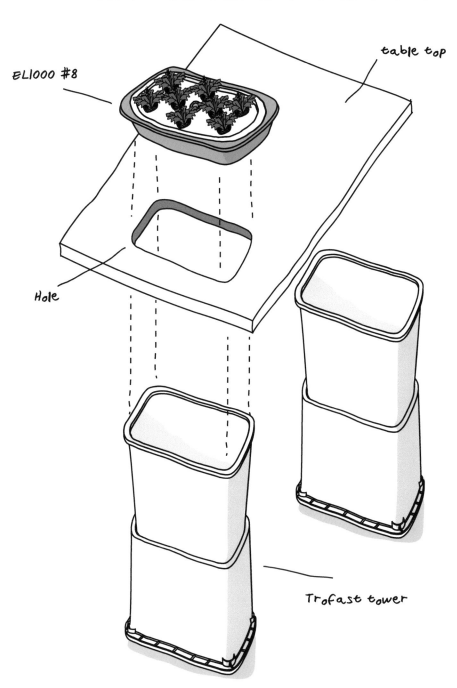

ELI000 #8

table top

Hole

Trofast tower

A PLACE THE TROFAST "TOWER" UNDER THE TABLE TOP. FROM THE TOP, YOU SHOULD NOT BE ABLE TO SEE THE EDGES OF THE BOX THROUGH THE HOLE YOU CUT IN THE BOARD.

BEFORE FIXING IT, GO TO STEP B.

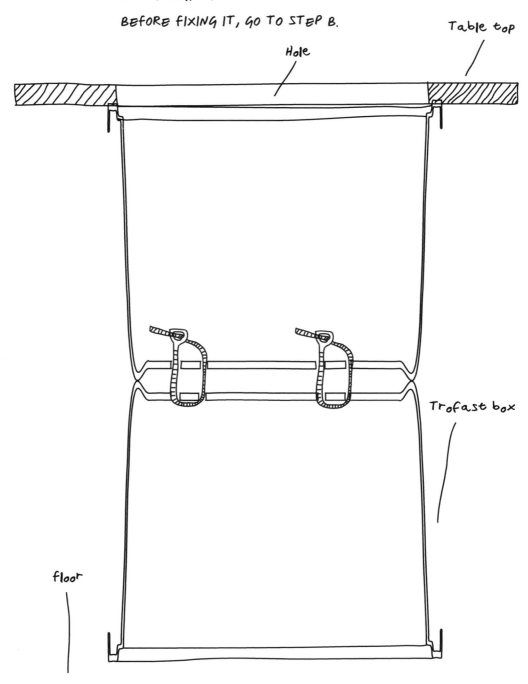

Hole

Table top

Trofast box

floor

B MAKE SURE YOU CAN INSERT AN ELI000 8 INTO THE OPENING. THE EDGES OF THE BOX SHOULD BE ABLE TO COVER THE ROUGH EDGES OF THE WOOD. YOU CAN LIFT IT OUT WHENEVER YOU WANT AND YOU CAN USE THE SPACE UNDERNEATH TO STORE GARDENING EQUIPMENT.

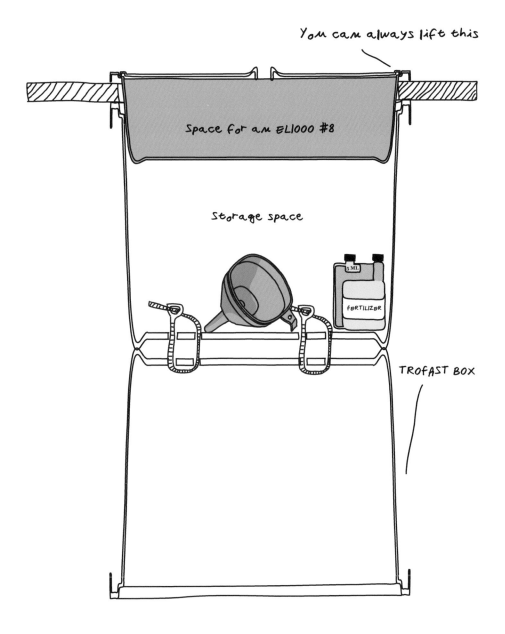

You can always lift this

Space for an ELI000 #8

Storage space

5 ML

FERTILIZER

TROFAST BOX

C TURN THE TABLE
UPSIDE DOWN AND
FIX THE BOXES TO THE
TABLE TOP WITH FOUR
SCREWS FOR EACH BOX.
THIS WILL ADD
STABILITY TO THE
TABLE.

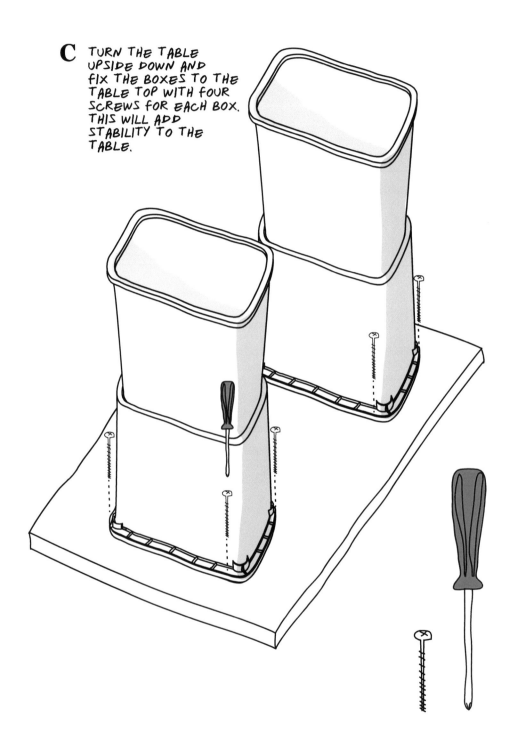

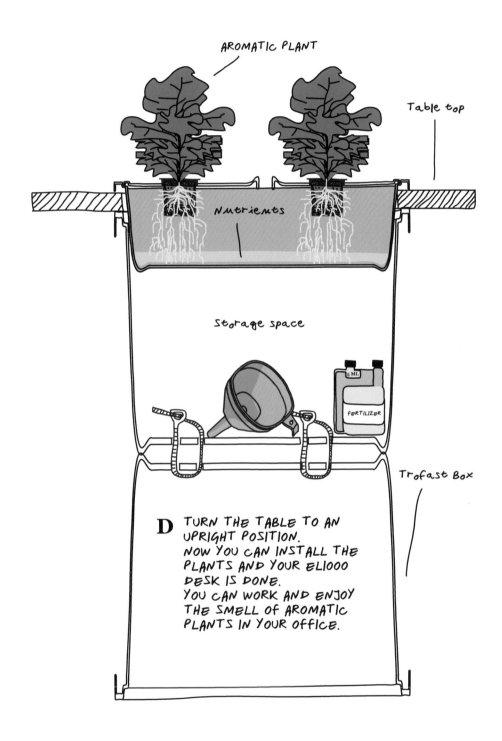

AROMATIC PLANT

Table top

Nutrients

Storage space

5 ML

FERTILIZER

Trofast Box

D TURN THE TABLE TO AN UPRIGHT POSITION.
NOW YOU CAN INSTALL THE PLANTS AND YOUR ELIOOO DESK IS DONE.
YOU CAN WORK AND ENJOY THE SMELL OF AROMATIC PLANTS IN YOUR OFFICE.

ELIOOO OFFICE

ELIOOO #30

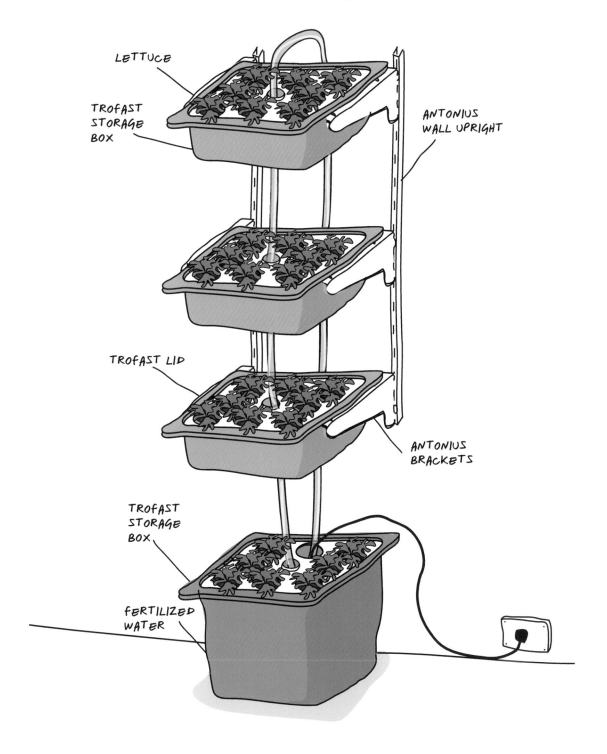

LETTUCE

TROFAST
STORAGE
BOX

ANTONIUS
WALL UPRIGHT

TROFAST LID

ANTONIUS
BRACKETS

TROFAST
STORAGE
BOX

FERTILIZED
WATER

ELIOOO #30 WHAT YOU NEED
FROM IKEA

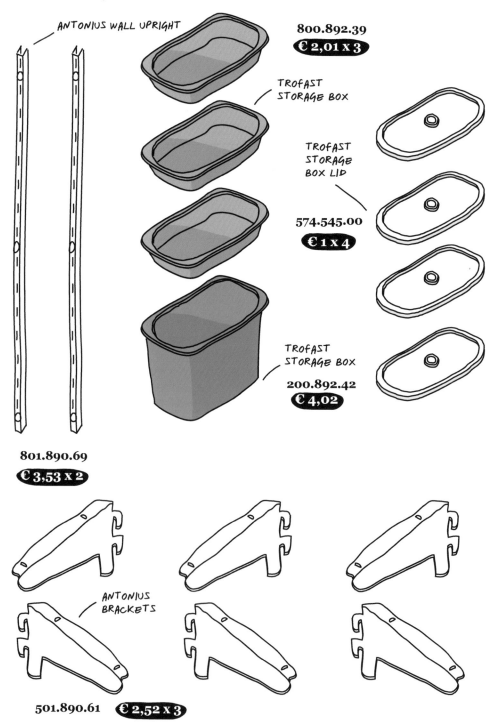

ANTONIUS WALL UPRIGHT

800.892.39

€ 2,01 x 3

TROFAST
STORAGE BOX

TROFAST
STORAGE
BOX LID

574.545.00

€ 1 x 4

TROFAST
STORAGE BOX

200.892.42

€ 4,02

801.890.69

€ 3,53 x 2

ANTONIUS
BRACKETS

501.890.61   € 2,52 x 3

FROM A GARDENING SHOP

Net pot ⌀ 5 cm

OTHER SUPPLIES

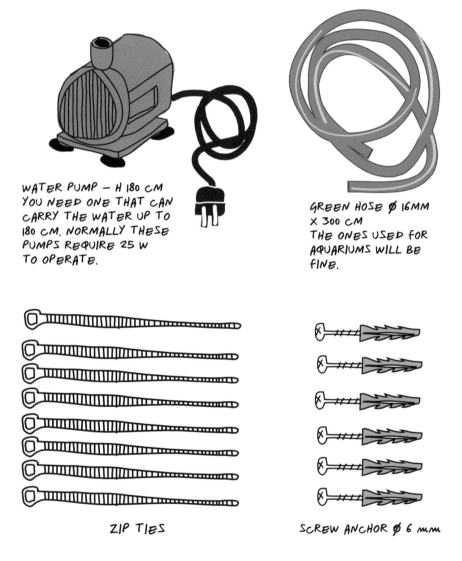

WATER PUMP — H 180 CM
YOU NEED ONE THAT CAN
CARRY THE WATER UP TO
180 CM. NORMALLY THESE
PUMPS REQUIRE 25 W
TO OPERATE.

GREEN HOSE Ø 16MM
X 300 CM
THE ONES USED FOR
AQUARIUMS WILL BE
FINE.

ZIP TIES

SCREW ANCHOR Ø 6 mm

TOOLS

14

6

3

50

1 POSITIONING

42

A MAKE TWO PENCIL
MARKS ON THE WALL
WHERE THE ANTONIUS
WALL UPRIGHTS WILL BE PLACED.
MAKE SURE THE MEASUREMENT
IS ACCURATE.
USE A LEVEL TO MARK POINTS ON
A STRAIGHT LINE.

WALL

164

B DRILL A Ø 6 MM HOLE INTO
THE WALL WHERE YOU MADE THE MARKS.
PLACE THE SCREW ANCHORS
OF THE SAME SIZE IN THE
HOLES.

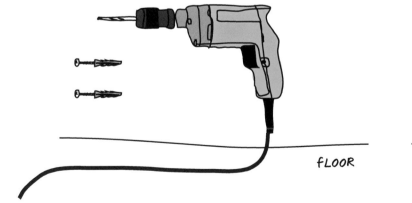

FLOOR

2 INSTALLING

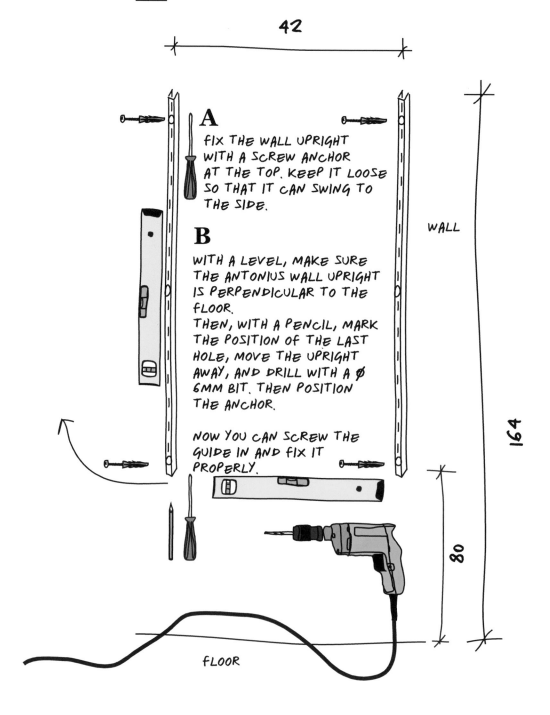

42

A

FIX THE WALL UPRIGHT WITH A SCREW ANCHOR AT THE TOP. KEEP IT LOOSE SO THAT IT CAN SWING TO THE SIDE.

B

WITH A LEVEL, MAKE SURE THE ANTONIUS WALL UPRIGHT IS PERPENDICULAR TO THE FLOOR.
THEN, WITH A PENCIL, MARK THE POSITION OF THE LAST HOLE, MOVE THE UPRIGHT AWAY, AND DRILL WITH A ⌀ 6MM BIT. THEN POSITION THE ANCHOR.

NOW YOU CAN SCREW THE GUIDE IN AND FIX IT PROPERLY.

WALL

164

80

FLOOR

3 ATTATCHING THE BRACKETS

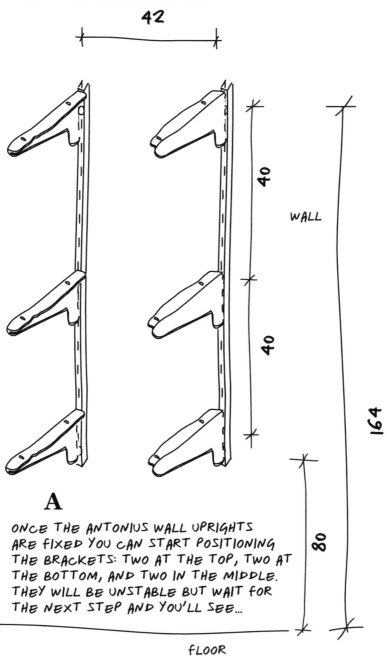

A

ONCE THE ANTONIUS WALL UPRIGHTS
ARE FIXED YOU CAN START POSITIONING
THE BRACKETS: TWO AT THE TOP, TWO AT
THE BOTTOM, AND TWO IN THE MIDDLE.
THEY WILL BE UNSTABLE BUT WAIT FOR
THE NEXT STEP AND YOU'LL SEE...

42

40

40

WALL

164

80

FLOOR

4 PREPARING THE GROW TRAYS

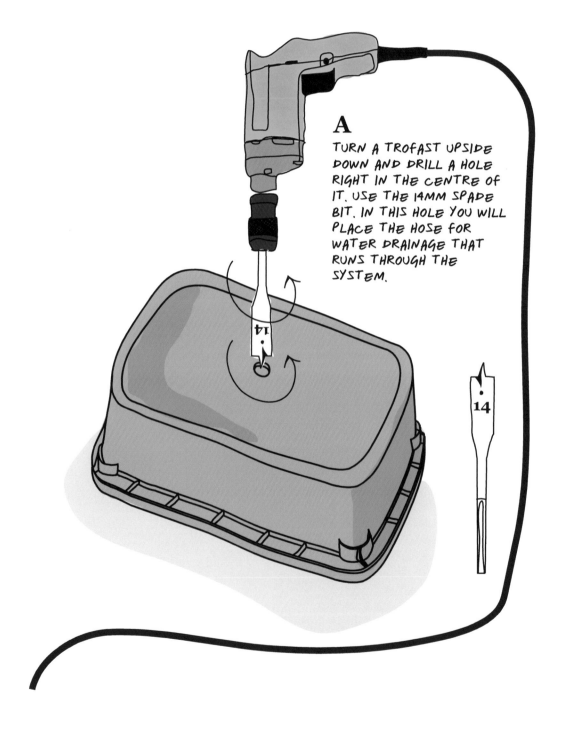

A

TURN A TROFAST UPSIDE DOWN AND DRILL A HOLE RIGHT IN THE CENTRE OF IT. USE THE 14MM SPADE BIT. IN THIS HOLE YOU WILL PLACE THE HOSE FOR WATER DRAINAGE THAT RUNS THROUGH THE SYSTEM.

B

MARK EIGHT SPOTS ON THE TROFAST LID
WITH A PENCIL.

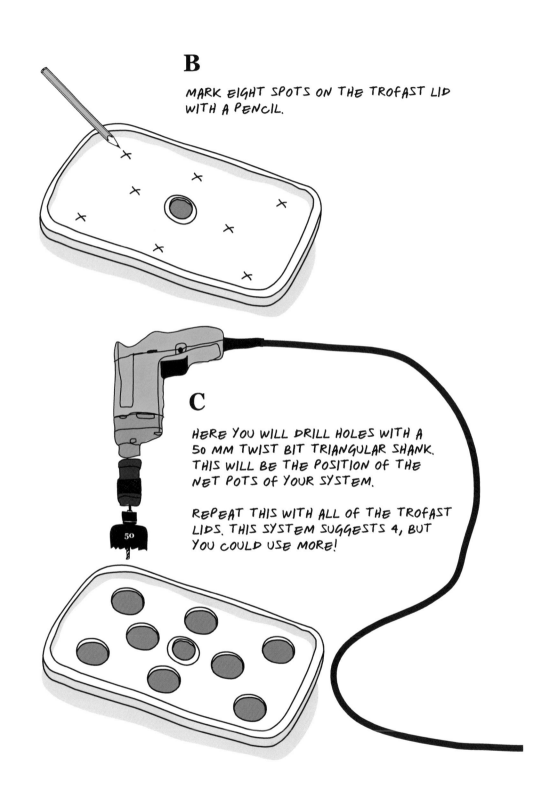

C

HERE YOU WILL DRILL HOLES WITH A
50 MM TWIST BIT TRIANGULAR SHANK.
THIS WILL BE THE POSITION OF THE
NET POTS OF YOUR SYSTEM.

REPEAT THIS WITH ALL OF THE TROFAST
LIDS. THIS SYSTEM SUGGESTS 4, BUT
YOU COULD USE MORE!

D

MAKE A MARK IN THE WIDTH OF THE TROFAST BOX, AT THE MID POINT NEXT TO THE HOLE THAT ALREADY EXISTS. HERE DRILL A HOLE WITH A 3 MM BIT. YOU WILL NEED THIS HOLE TO TIE THE BOX WITH A ZIP TIE TO THE BRACKETS.

3

TROFAST STORAGE BOX

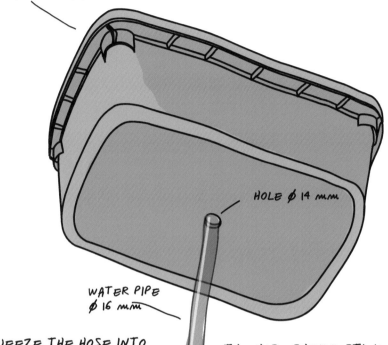

HOLE ⌀ 14 mm

WATER PIPE
⌀ 16 mm

E

SQUEEZE THE HOSE INTO
THE HOLE DRILLED WITH
THE SPADE BIT.
THE HOLE IS ⌀ 14 MM
WHILE THE PIPE IS 16 MM.
THIS DIFFERENCE WILL
PREVENT LEAKAGE
AROUND THE PIPE. YOU
MIGHT USE SOME DISH
SOAP AS LUBRICANT.
THIS PROCESS MIGHT BE A
BIT TEDIOUS, BUT IT
WORKS.
REPEAT THIS IN ALL THREE
TRAYS IN THIS SYSTEM.

THE HOSE SHOULD STICK
OUT FROM THE BOTTOM OF
THE TROFAST FOR NO MORE
THAN 2-3 CM.
THIS LENGTH DETERMINES
THE WATER LEVEL IN EACH
TRAY. TECHNICALLY, YOU
WOULD NOT NEED MUCH OF
IT. JUST A SMALL STREAM
WOULD BE ENOUGH.

5 MOUNTING THE GROW TRAYS

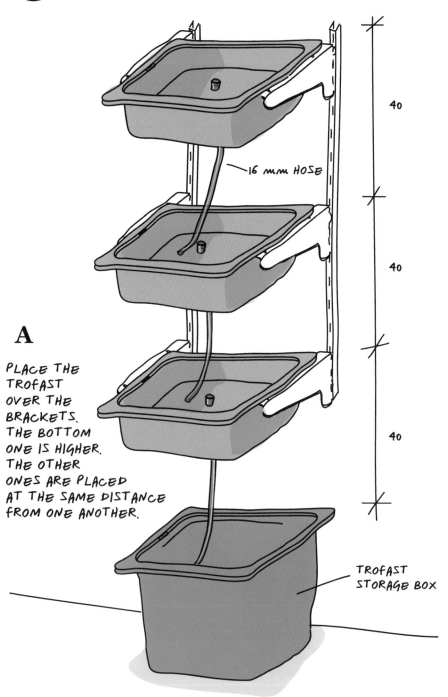

16 mm HOSE

40

40

40

A

PLACE THE
TROFAST
OVER THE
BRACKETS.
THE BOTTOM
ONE IS HIGHER.
THE OTHER
ONES ARE PLACED
AT THE SAME DISTANCE
FROM ONE ANOTHER.

TROFAST
STORAGE BOX

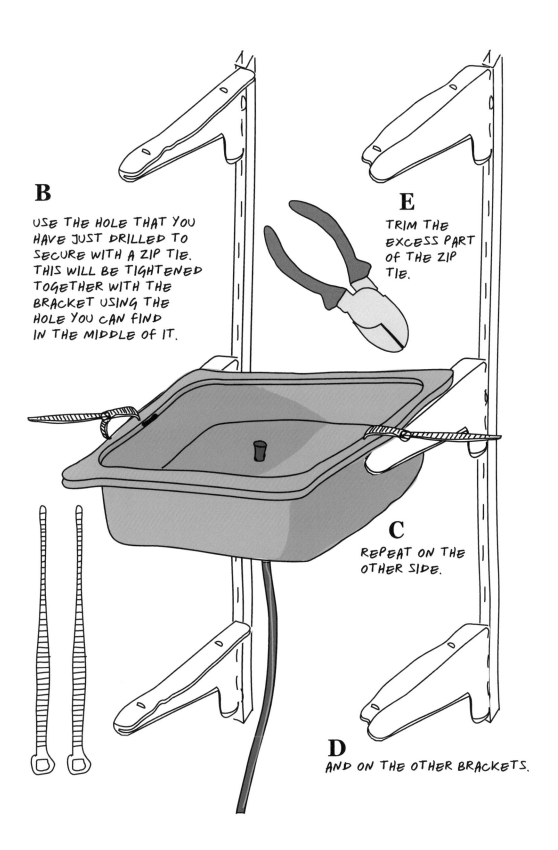

B

USE THE HOLE THAT YOU
HAVE JUST DRILLED TO
SECURE WITH A ZIP TIE.
THIS WILL BE TIGHTENED
TOGETHER WITH THE
BRACKET USING THE
HOLE YOU CAN FIND
IN THE MIDDLE OF IT.

E

TRIM THE
EXCESS PART
OF THE ZIP
TIE.

C

REPEAT ON THE
OTHER SIDE.

D

AND ON THE OTHER BRACKETS.

6 PPP
pumps, plants, and pipes

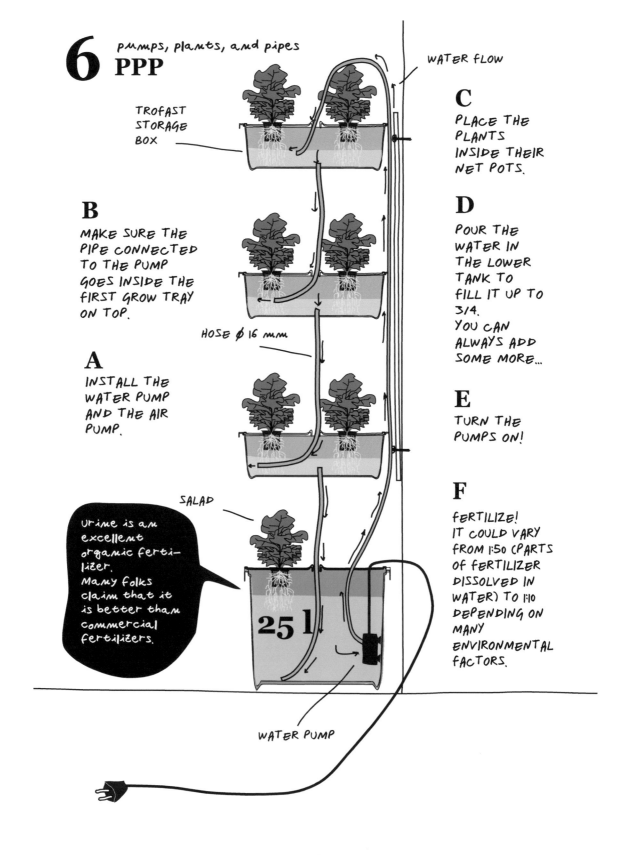

TROFAST STORAGE BOX

WATER FLOW

B

MAKE SURE THE PIPE CONNECTED TO THE PUMP GOES INSIDE THE FIRST GROW TRAY ON TOP.

HOSE Ø 16 mm

A

INSTALL THE WATER PUMP AND THE AIR PUMP.

SALAD

Urine is an excellent organic fertilizer. Many folks claim that it is better than commercial fertilizers.

25 l

WATER PUMP

C

PLACE THE PLANTS INSIDE THEIR NET POTS.

D

POUR THE WATER IN THE LOWER TANK TO FILL IT UP TO 3/4. YOU CAN ALWAYS ADD SOME MORE...

E

TURN THE PUMPS ON!

F

FERTILIZE! IT COULD VARY FROM 1:50 (PARTS OF FERTILIZER DISSOLVED IN WATER) TO 1:10 DEPENDING ON MANY ENVIRONMENTAL FACTORS.

7 INSTALLING THE NET POTS

INSERT THE WATER PIPE THROUGH THE HOLE IN THE LID. THIS WOULD MAKE IT EASY TO REMOVE, WHEN CLEANING OR HAR-VESTING, FOR INSTANCE.

ALL THE OTHER TECHNICAL PARTS INCLUDING THE WATER HOSE CAN GO OUT FROM THIS NET POT HOLE IN THE TROFAST BOX THAT IS USED HERE AS A WATER TANK.

AT THIS POINT IT IS POSSIBLE TO PLACE THE NET POTS INTO THE GROWING TRAYS. THESE WILL NOT HAVE TO BE IN DIRECT CONTACT WITH THE WATER. RATHER, THE ROOTS WILL GROW TOWARDS IT.

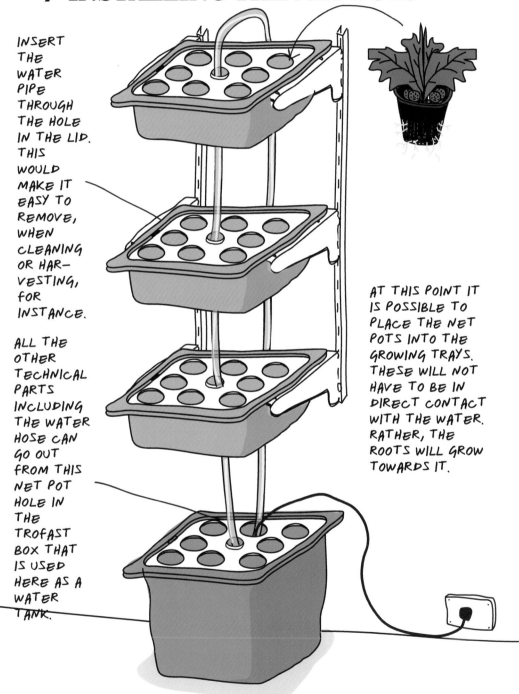

ENJOY

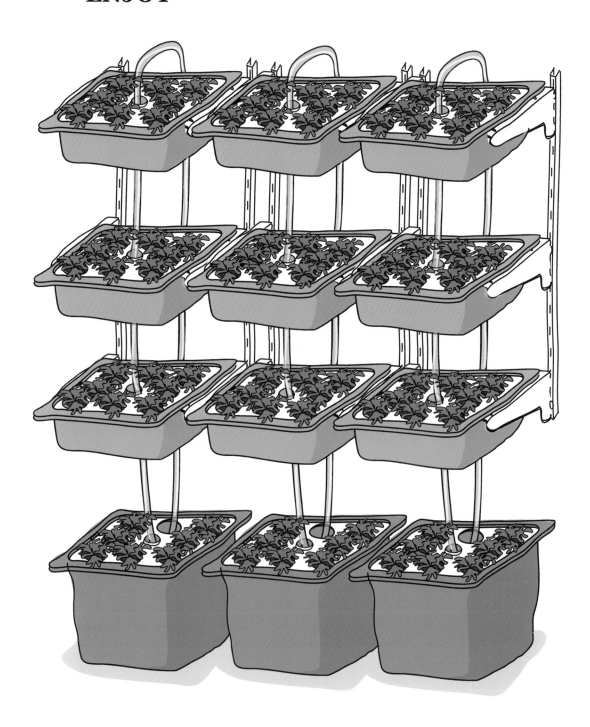

ELIOOO #30 Mobile

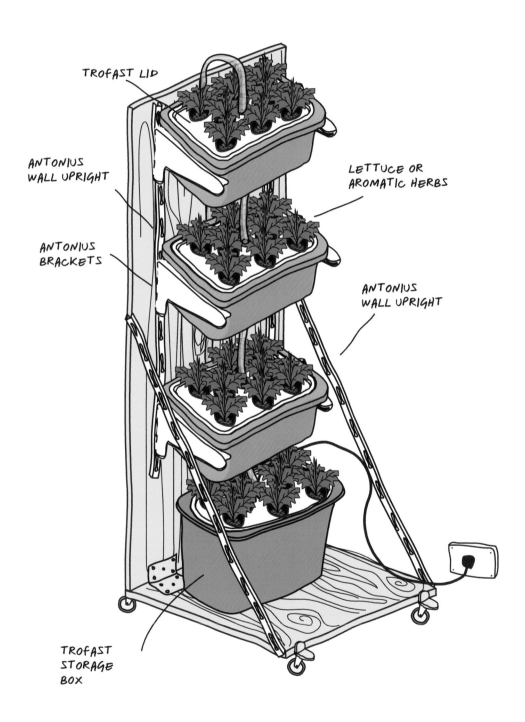

TROFAST LID

ANTONIUS WALL UPRIGHT

ANTONIUS BRACKETS

LETTUCE OR AROMATIC HERBS

ANTONIUS WALL UPRIGHT

TROFAST STORAGE BOX

ELIOOO #30 Mobile. WHAT YOU NEED

FROM IKEA

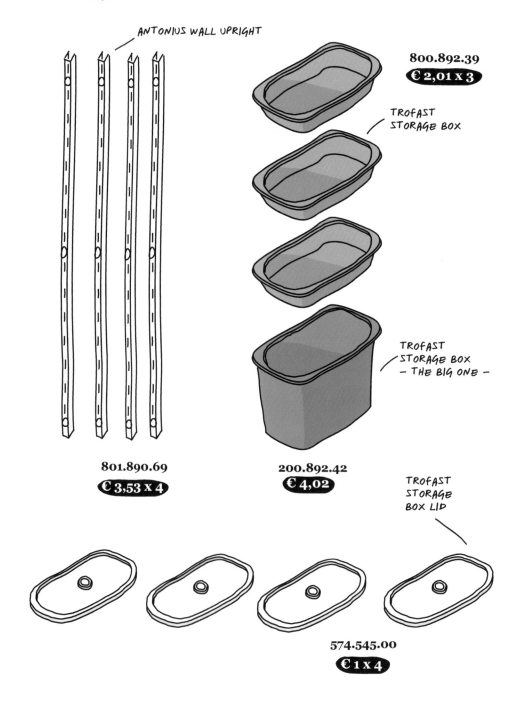

ANTONIUS WALL UPRIGHT

800.892.39
€ 2,01 x 3

TROFAST
STORAGE BOX

TROFAST
STORAGE BOX
– THE BIG ONE –

801.890.69
€ 3,53 x 4

200.892.42
€ 4,02

TROFAST
STORAGE
BOX LID

574.545.00
€ 1 x 4

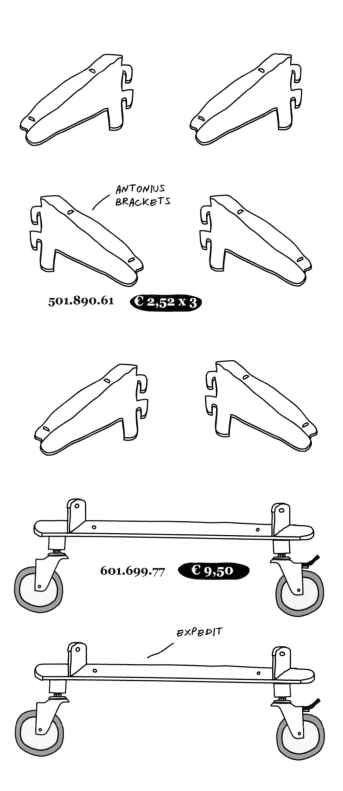

ANTONIUS
BRACKETS

501.890.61 **€ 2,52 x 3**

601.699.77 **€ 9,50**

EXPEDIT

119

FROM A GARDENING SHOP

Net pot ⌀ 5 cm

Expanded clay

Grow Starter

OTHER SUPPLIES

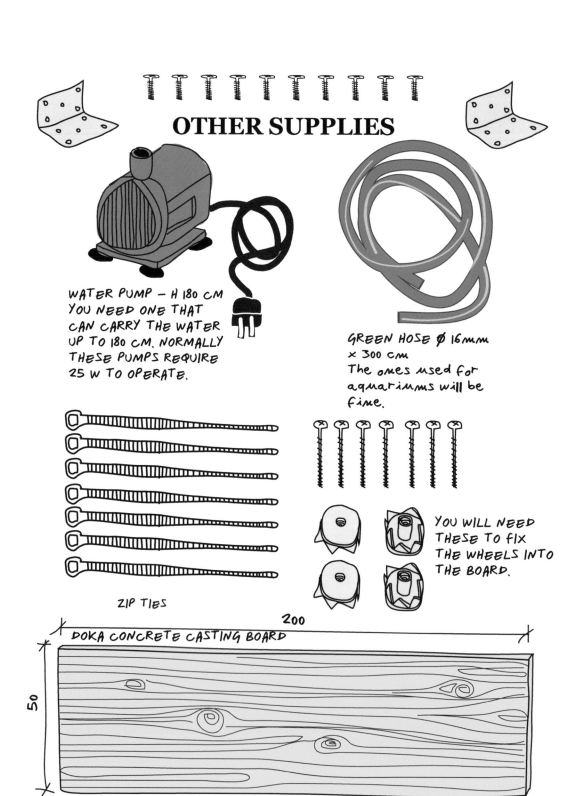

WATER PUMP — H 180 CM
YOU NEED ONE THAT
CAN CARRY THE WATER
UP TO 180 CM. NORMALLY
THESE PUMPS REQUIRE
25 W TO OPERATE.

GREEN HOSE Ø 16mm
x 300 cm
The ones used for
aquariums will be
fine.

YOU WILL NEED
THESE TO FIX
THE WHEELS INTO
THE BOARD.

ZIP TIES

200

50

DOKA CONCRETE CASTING BOARD

DO YOU WANT TO GO OFF GRID?
A SOLAR POND PUMP SET COULD DO THAT.
JUST MAKE SURE IT CAN CARRY THE
WATER UP TO 160 CM.

TOOLS

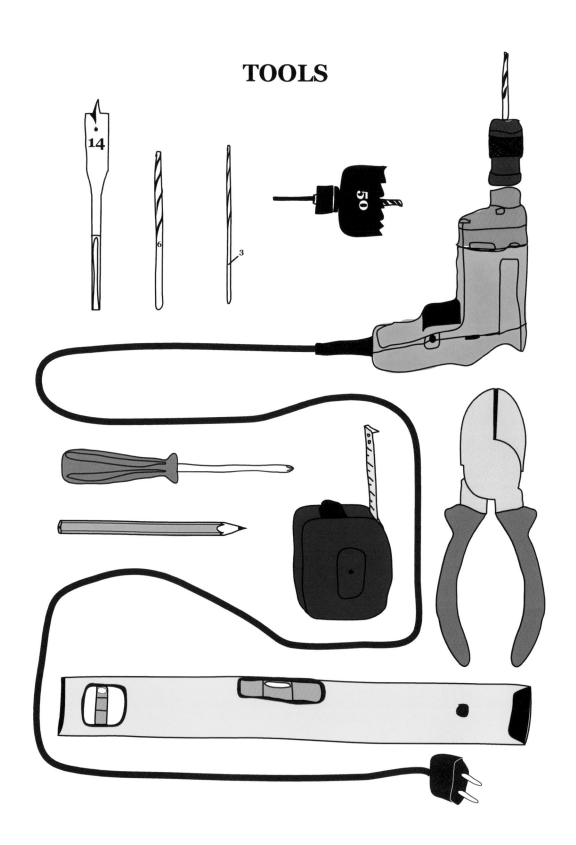

1 PREPARING THE ELIOOO BOARD

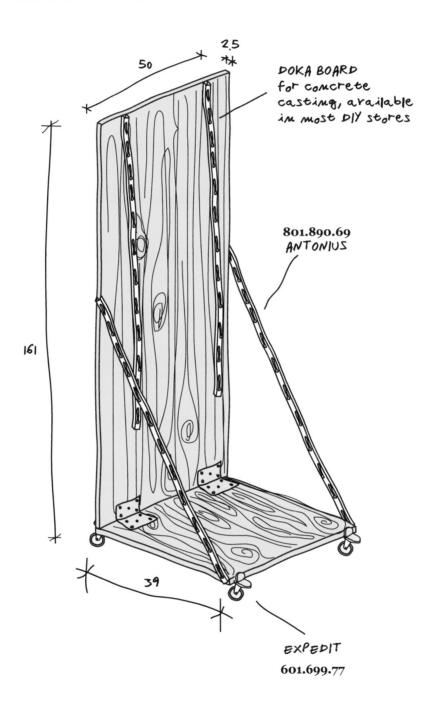

2.5

50

DOKA BOARD
for concrete
casting, available
in most DIY stores

801.890.69
ANTONIUS

161

39

EXPEDIT
601.699.77

DOKA CONCRETE CASTING BOARD

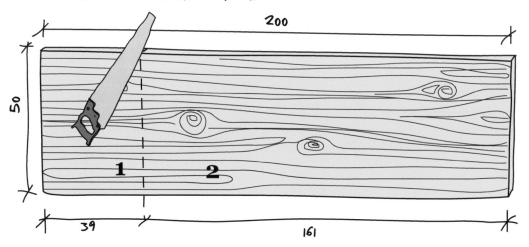

200

50

39

161

A

BUY A DOKA BOARD. NORMALLY
THESE ARE SOLD 200 CM X 50
CM. THESE ARE PERFECT FOR
THIS PURPOSE BECAUSE THE
WOOD RESISTS HUMIDITY. YOU
CAN ASK AN EMPLOYEE OF
THE DIY SHOP TO CUT THE
BOARD FOR YOU.

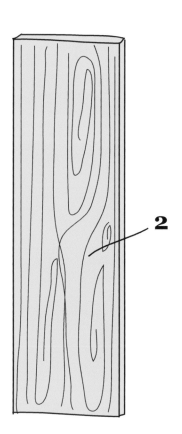

2

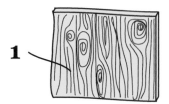

1

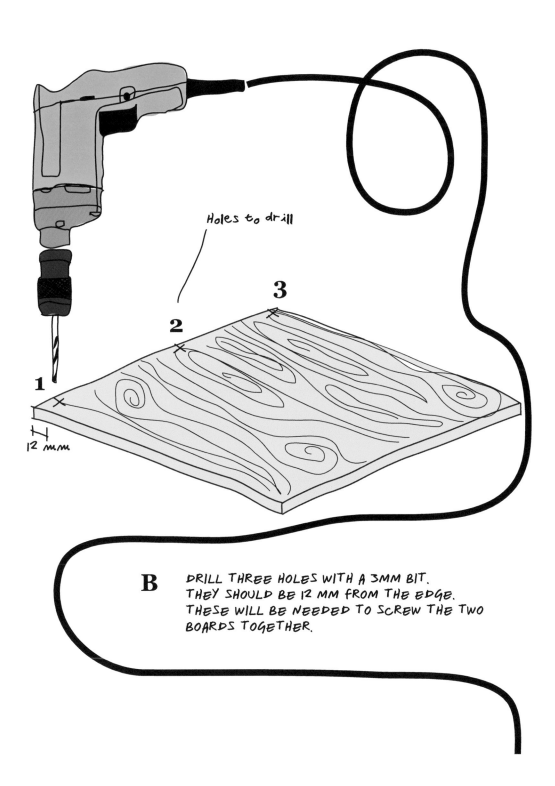

Holes to drill

1   2   3

12 mm

B DRILL THREE HOLES WITH A 3MM BIT.
THEY SHOULD BE 12 MM FROM THE EDGE.
THESE WILL BE NEEDED TO SCREW THE TWO
BOARDS TOGETHER.

C1

PLACE THE WHEELS ON TOP OF THE BASE.

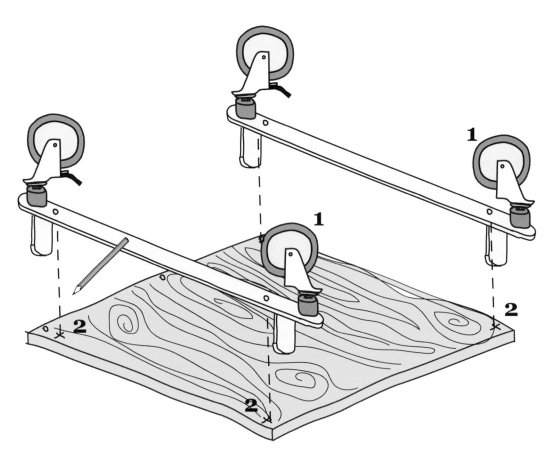

C2

MARK THE SPOTS FOR THE HOLES TO BE DRILLED.

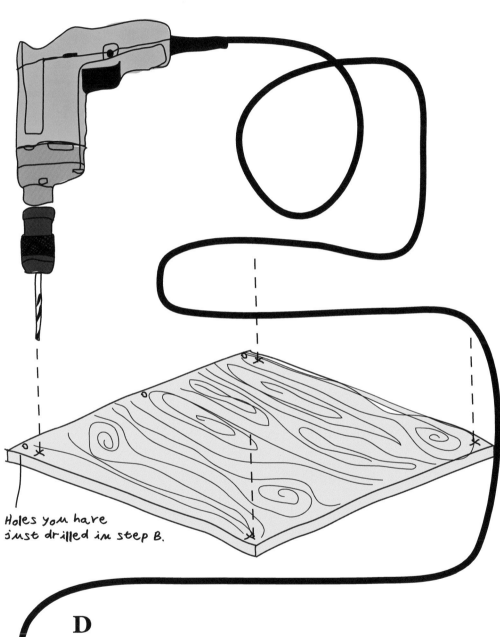

Holes you have just drilled in step B.

D

DRILL HOLES IN THE BOARD ON THE SPOTS YOU MARKED IN C2.

E

INSERT THE SCREWS THROUGH THE HOLES YOU HAVE ALREADY DRILLED. THIS IS THE FIRST STEP IN JOINING THE TWO BOARDS TOGETHER.

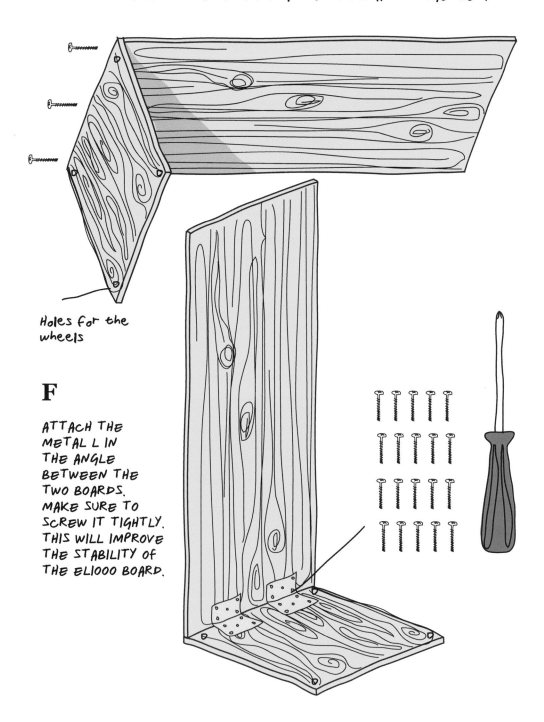

Holes for the wheels

F

ATTACH THE METAL L IN THE ANGLE BETWEEN THE TWO BOARDS. MAKE SURE TO SCREW IT TIGHTLY. THIS WILL IMPROVE THE STABILITY OF THE EL1000 BOARD.

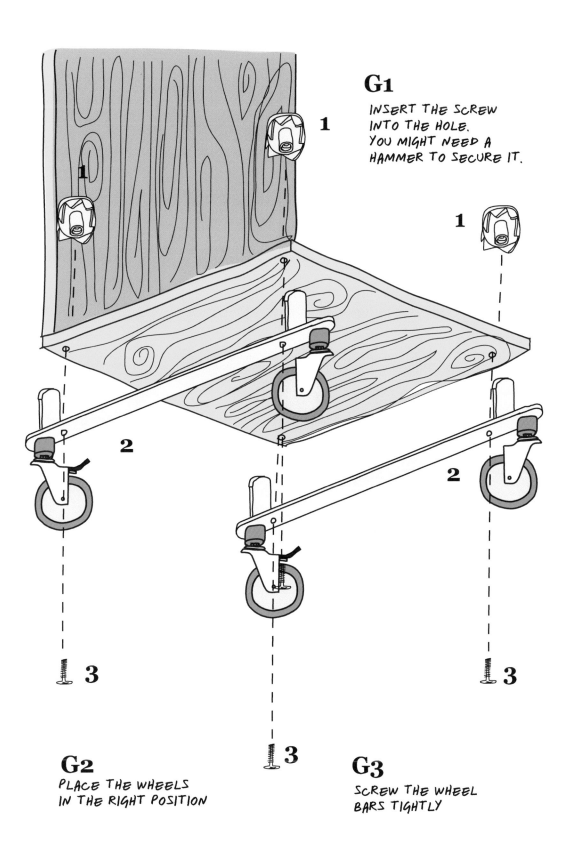

G1
INSERT THE SCREW
INTO THE HOLE.
YOU MIGHT NEED A
HAMMER TO SECURE IT.

G2
PLACE THE WHEELS
IN THE RIGHT POSITION

G3
SCREW THE WHEEL
BARS TIGHTLY

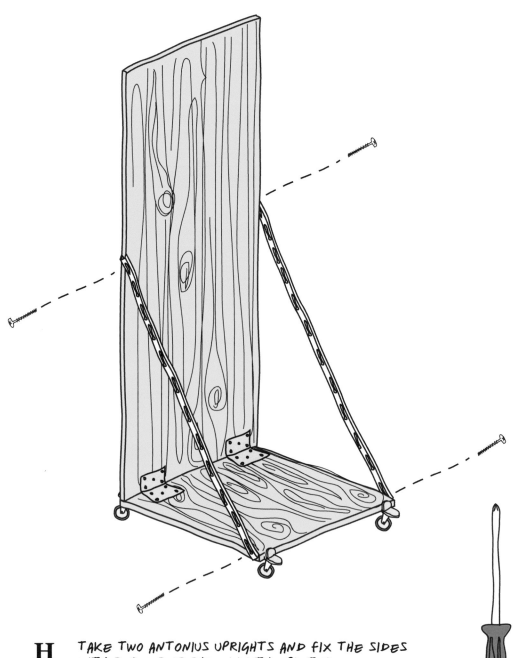

H   TAKE TWO ANTONIUS UPRIGHTS AND FIX THE SIDES
WITH SCREWS AS SHOWN IN THE PICTURE.
THIS WILL COMPLETE THE ELIOOO #30 MOBILE BOARD AND
IT WILL BE STABLE ENOUGH TO SUPPORT THE GROW
TRAYS.

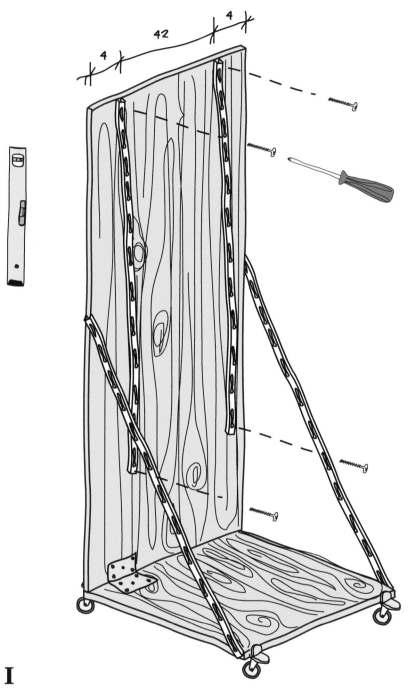

I FIX THE ANTONIUS BRACKET ON THE BACK OF THE
EL1000 BOARD. MAKE SURE THEY ARE STRAIGHT, CENTRED,
AND 42 CM ONE FROM THE OTHER. USE A WATER LEVEL TO MAKE SURE
THEY ARE PERFECTLY STRAIGHT AND PARALLEL TO EACH OTHER.

2 PREPARING THE GROW TRAYS

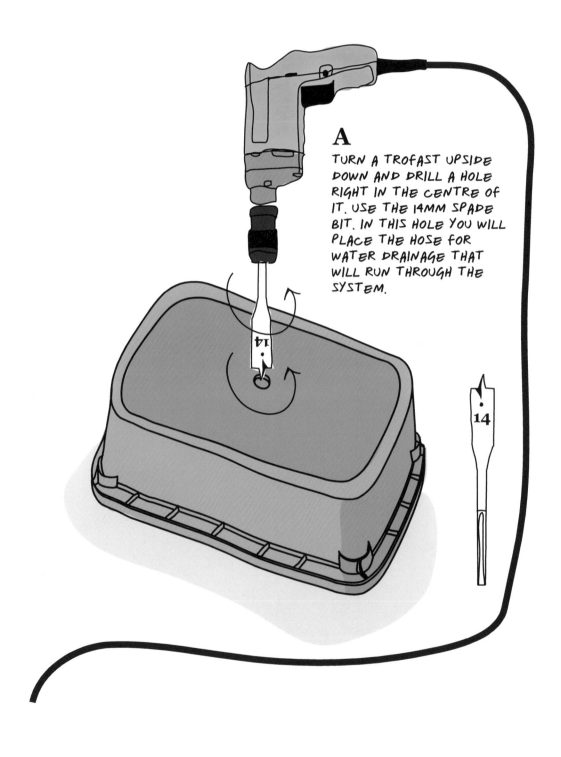

A

TURN A TROFAST UPSIDE
DOWN AND DRILL A HOLE
RIGHT IN THE CENTRE OF
IT. USE THE 14MM SPADE
BIT. IN THIS HOLE YOU WILL
PLACE THE HOSE FOR
WATER DRAINAGE THAT
WILL RUN THROUGH THE
SYSTEM.

B

MARK EIGHT SPOTS ON THE TROFAST
LID WITH A PENCIL.

C

HERE, DRILL HOLES WITH A
50 MM TWIST BIT TRIANGULAR SHANK.
THIS WILL BE THE POSITION OF THE
NET POTS IN YOUR SYSTEM.

REPEAT THIS WITH ALL THE TROFAST LIDS.
THIS SYSTEM SUGGESTS 4, BUT YOU
COULD MAKE MORE!

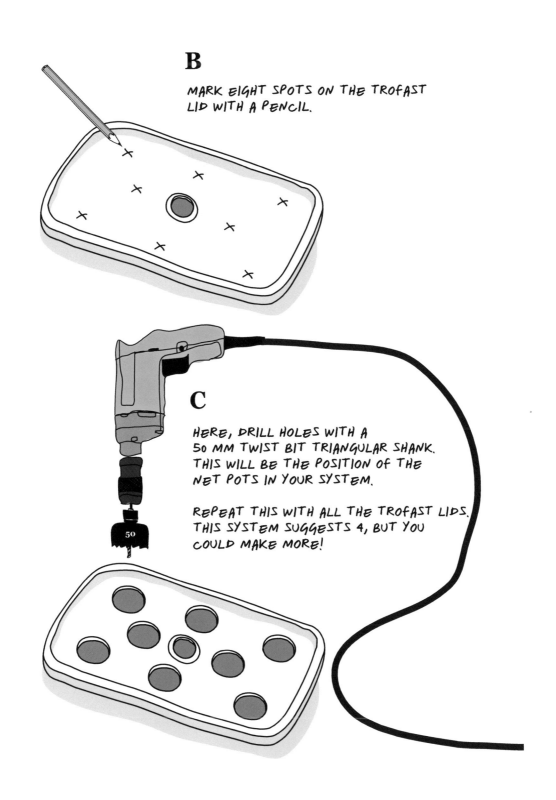

D

MAKE A MARK IN THE MIDDLE OF THE TROFAST BOX, NEXT TO THE HOLE THAT ALREADY EXISTS. HERE, DRILL A HOLE WITH A 3 MM BIT. YOU WILL NEED THIS HOLE TO TIE THE BOX TO THE BRACKETS WITH A ZIP TIE.

3

TROFAST STORAGE BOX

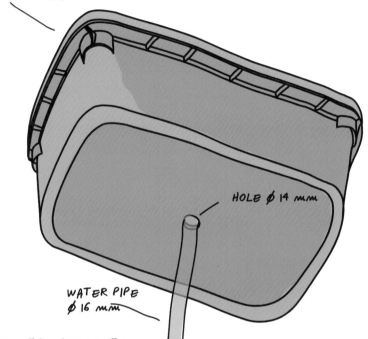

HOLE ⌀ 14 mm

WATER PIPE
⌀ 16 mm

E

SQUEEZE THE HOSE INTO
THE HOLE DRILLED WITH
THE SPADE BIT.
THE HOLE IS ⌀ 14 MM
WHILE THE PIPE IS 16 MM.
THIS GAP BETWEEN THE
TWO WILL CREATE A
PRESSURE PREVENTING
WATER FROM LEAKING
FROM THE PIPE. YOU MIGHT
USE SOME DISH SOAP TO
FACILITATE THE PEN-
ETRATION.
THIS PROCESS MIGHT BE A
BIT TEDIOUS BUT IT WORKS.
REPEAT THIS IN ALL THREE
TRAYS IN THIS SYSTEM.

THE HOSE, HOWEVER,
SHOULD STICK OUT FROM
THE BOTTOM OF THE
TROFAST FOR NO MORE THAN
2-3 CM.
WITH THIS YOU CAN
REGULATE THE WATER
LEVEL IN EACH TRAY.
TECHNICALLY YOU WOULD
NOT NEED MUCH, JUST A
THIN STREAM WOULD BE
ENOUGH.

3 INSTALLING THE GROW TRAYS

THESE POINTS ARE
SIMILAR TO THE
ELI000 #30. HOWEVER,
I WILL REPEAT THEM
HERE FOR YOUR
CONVENIENCE.

A

ONCE THE
ANTONIUS WALL
UPRIGHTS ARE
FIXED YOU CAN
START POSITIONING
THE BRACKETS:
TWO AT
THE TOP, TWO AT
THE BOTTOM AND
TWO IN THE
MIDDLE. THEY WILL
STILL BE
UNSTABLE, BUT
WAIT FOR THE
NEXT STEP AND
YOU'LL SEE...

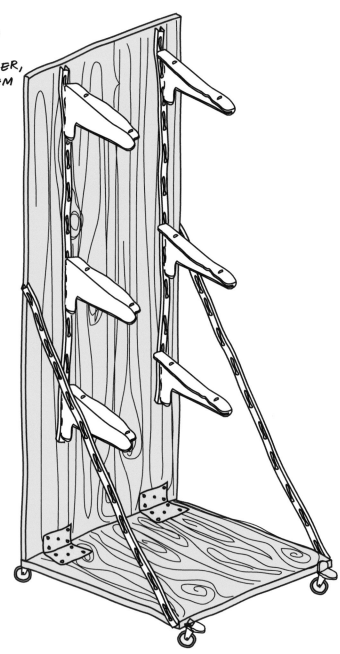

138

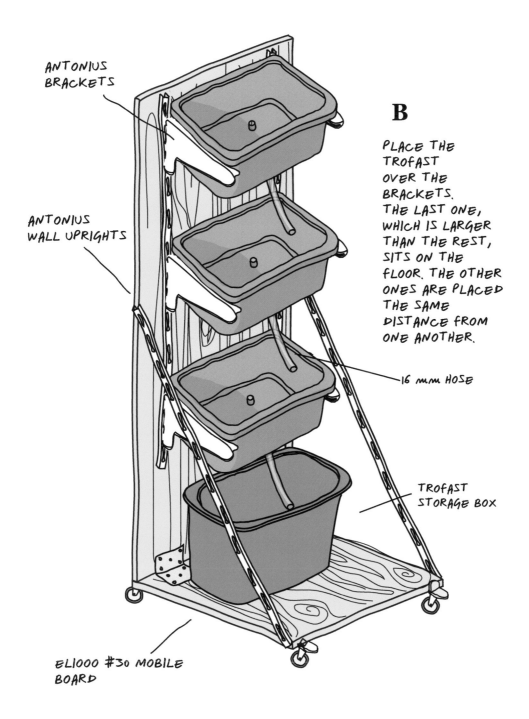

ANTONIUS
BRACKETS

ANTONIUS
WALL UPRIGHTS

EL1000 #30 MOBILE
BOARD

B

PLACE THE
TROFAST
OVER THE
BRACKETS.
THE LAST ONE,
WHICH IS LARGER
THAN THE REST,
SITS ON THE
FLOOR. THE OTHER
ONES ARE PLACED
THE SAME
DISTANCE FROM
ONE ANOTHER.

16 mm HOSE

TROFAST
STORAGE BOX

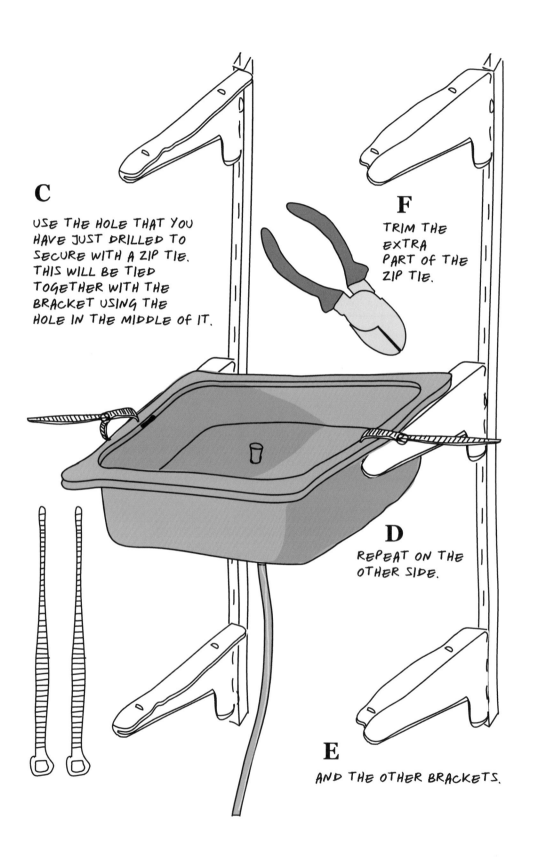

C

USE THE HOLE THAT YOU
HAVE JUST DRILLED TO
SECURE WITH A ZIP TIE.
THIS WILL BE TIED
TOGETHER WITH THE
BRACKET USING THE
HOLE IN THE MIDDLE OF IT.

F

TRIM THE
EXTRA
PART OF THE
ZIP TIE.

D

REPEAT ON THE
OTHER SIDE.

E

AND THE OTHER BRACKETS.

4

PPP
PUMPS, PLANTS, AND PIPES

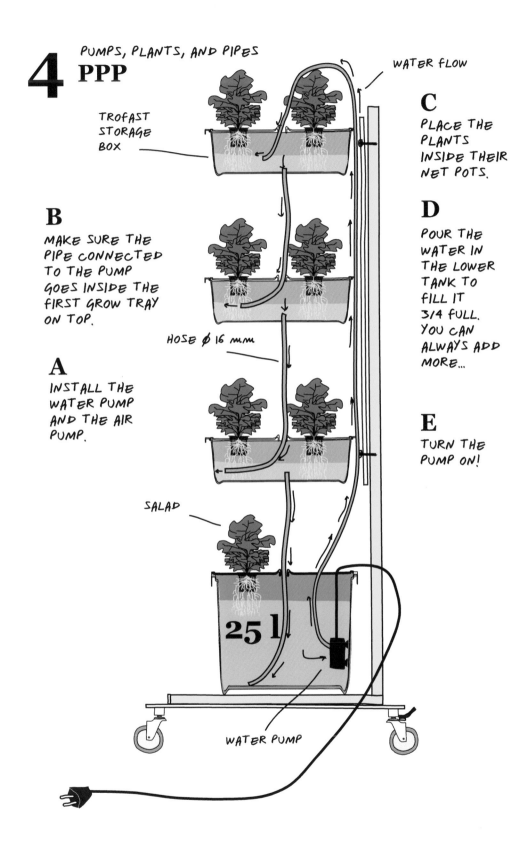

TROFAST
STORAGE
BOX

WATER FLOW

C

PLACE THE
PLANTS
INSIDE THEIR
NET POTS.

B

MAKE SURE THE
PIPE CONNECTED
TO THE PUMP
GOES INSIDE THE
FIRST GROW TRAY
ON TOP.

D

POUR THE
WATER IN
THE LOWER
TANK TO
FILL IT
3/4 FULL.
YOU CAN
ALWAYS ADD
MORE...

HOSE ⌀ 16 mm

A

INSTALL THE
WATER PUMP
AND THE AIR
PUMP.

E

TURN THE
PUMP ON!

SALAD

25 l

WATER PUMP

5 INSTALLING THE NET POTS

USE THE HOLE IN THE LID TO PLACE THE WATER PIPE. THIS ALLOWS IT TO BE EASILY REMOVED, WHEN CLEANING OR HARVESTING FOR INSTANCE.

ALL THE OTHER TECHNICAL PARTS, INCLUDING THE WATER HOSE, CAN GO OUT FROM THIS NET POT HOLE IN THE TROFAST BOX THAT IS USED HERE AS A WATER TANK.

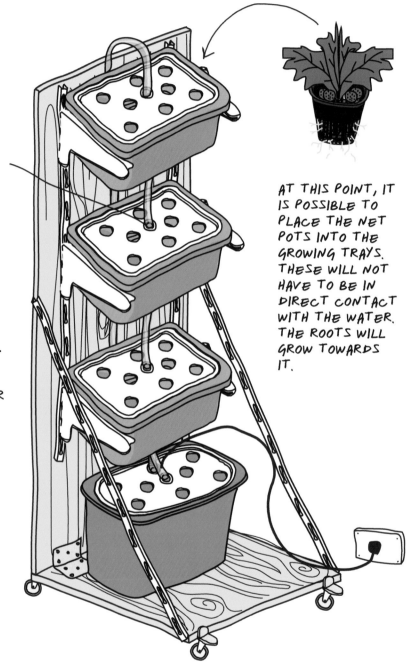

AT THIS POINT, IT IS POSSIBLE TO PLACE THE NET POTS INTO THE GROWING TRAYS. THESE WILL NOT HAVE TO BE IN DIRECT CONTACT WITH THE WATER. THE ROOTS WILL GROW TOWARDS IT.

ELIOOO #30
Mobile Off Grid

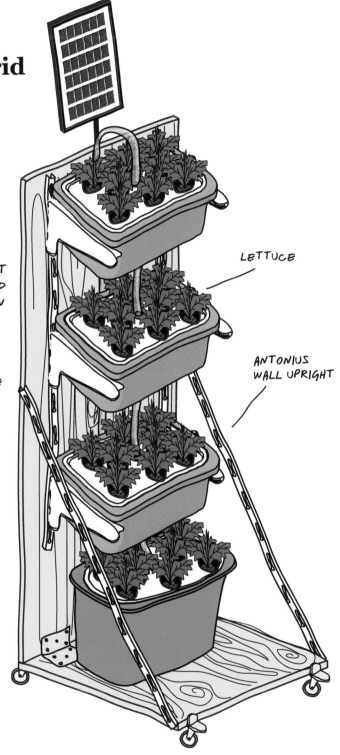

THERE ARE MANY
PHOTOVOLTAIC PANELS
AVAILABLE ON THE MARKET
TO CONNECT TO THE POND
PUMP. THESE WOULD ALLOW
YOU TO GO OFF GRID.
I CANNOT RECOMMEND
ANY SPECIFIC DEVICE AS
THEY CAN CHANGE AND
IMPROVE IN PERFORMANCE
SIGNIFICANTLY.
THEY CAN BE FIXED ON
TOP OF THE ELIOOO #30
BOARD, OR THEY CAN
BE PLACED ON THE SIDE
TO GET THE BEST
EXPOSURE TO
SUNLIGHT.

LETTUCE

ANTONIUS
WALL UPRIGHT

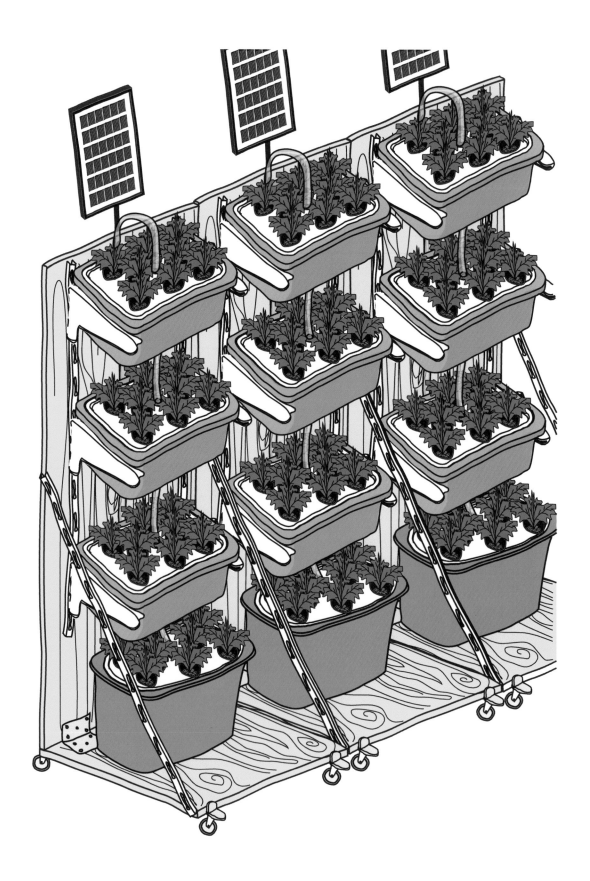

THIS IS ELIOOO #30 Mobile
AND IT CAN GROW TOMATOES

HERE IS HOW:

A FIX THE ANTONIUS BRACKET ON THE BACK OF THE EL1000 BOARD. MAKE SURE THEY ARE STRAIGHT, CENTRED, AND 42 CM APART.

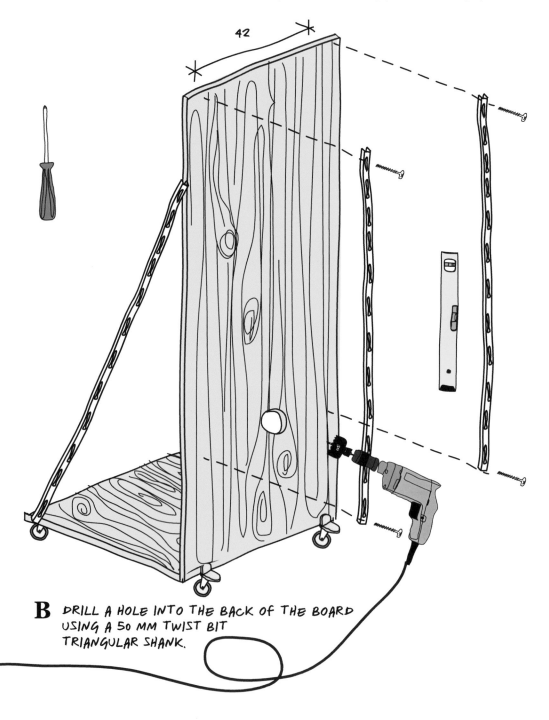

B DRILL A HOLE INTO THE BACK OF THE BOARD USING A 50 MM TWIST BIT TRIANGULAR SHANK.

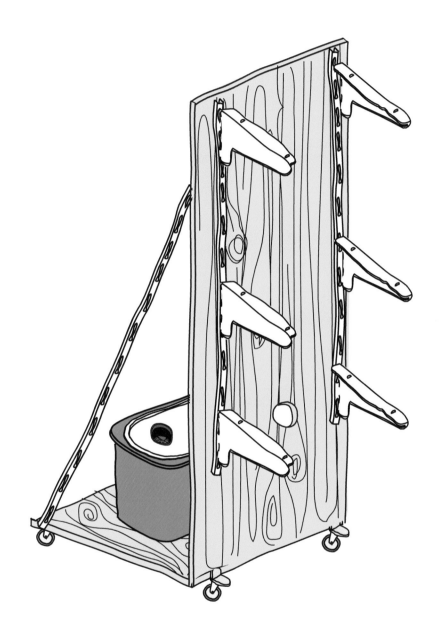

C   ASSEMBLE THE BRACKETS AND PLACE THE WATER TANK
FOR THE TOMATOES ON THE OTHER SIDE OF THE UNIT
FOR BETTER BALANCE.

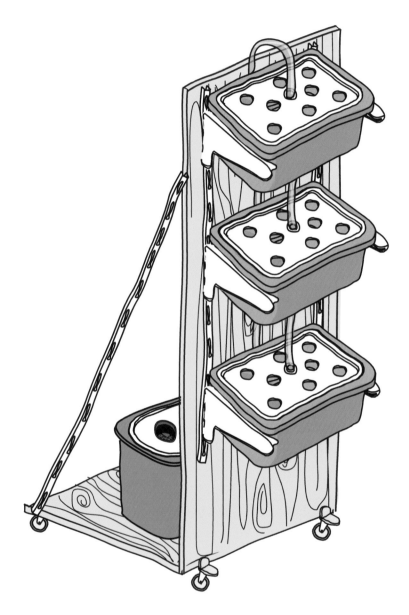

D FIX THE BOXES TO THE BRACKETS USING ZIP TIES AS
SHOWN IN STEPS B—C—D—E OF CHAPTER 5 OF ELIOOO #30 MOBILE.

E

THE TOMATOES CAN GROW STRAIGHT
UP AND BE TRAINED TO A TRELLIS
ON THE BOARD AS THEY GROW.
PLEASE NOTE THAT TOMATO PLANTS
REQUIRE MORE SPACE THAN AROMATIC
HERBS. MAKE SURE THEY HAVE ENOUGH
SPACE TO GROW.

HOSE ⌀ 16 mm

Lettuce

Tomatoes

TOMATOES REQUIRE
A LOT OF LIGHT
EVEN THOUGH THEY
PREFER INDIRECT
LIGHT. THE COOL THING
ABOUT THIS MOBILE
UNIT IS THAT YOU
CAN MOVE IT TO REACH
THE BEST LIGHT
CONDITIONS.

Water pump

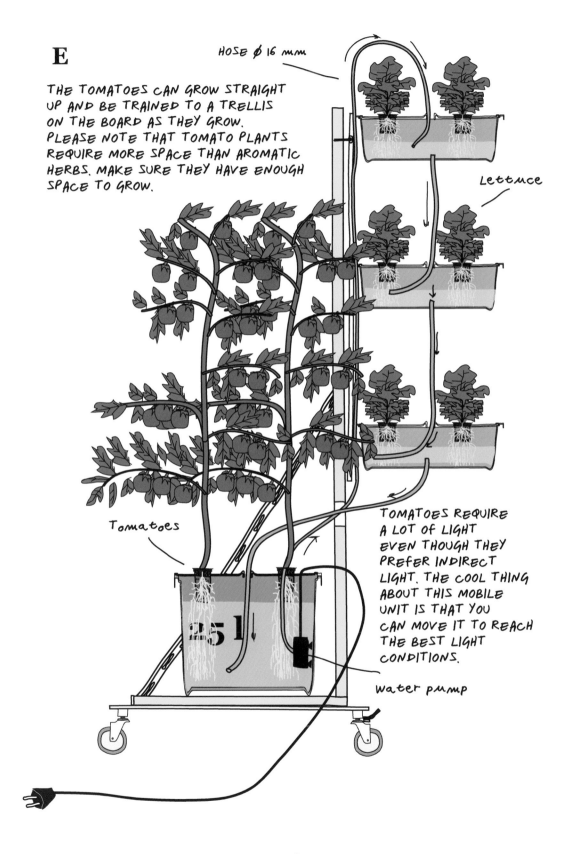

AFTERWARD

WHEN THIS BOOK WAS FIRST BEING DEVELOPED, I HAD INTENDED TO INCLUDE
SEVERAL ESSAYS BY OTHERS. AT THE TIME, I FELT THE NEED TO FRAME
THIS WORK WITHIN THE DISCOURSE OF THE CHALLENGES OF CONTEMPORARY
DESIGN. I ASKED SOME FRIENDS; AMBER HICKEY, TIDO VON OPPELN, AND
STEFANO MIRTI, WHO ARE VERY DEAR TO ME AND TO THIS WORK, TO WRITE A
PAGE OR TWO ABOUT IT. I THOUGHT FOR A LONG TIME ABOUT INCLUDING THEIR
WORDS IN THIS BOOK AND IN THE END, I DECIDED TO ONLY KEEP ONE SHORT
ESSAY. PERHAPS THESE OTHER ESSAYS WILL APPEAR IN AN EDITED VOLUME AT
A LATER DATE. I DECIDED THAT THIS IS NOT THE RIGHT PLATFORM FOR SUCH
A PROJECT. THIS BOOK IS ABOUT ELI000 AND IT SHOULD SPEAK FOR ITSELF
WITH ITS OWN VOICE.

THE ONE ESSAY ACCOMPANYING ELI000 IS BY ADRIAN NOTZ, THE DIRECTOR OF
CABARET VOLTAIRE, A SMALL BUT IMPORTANT INSTITUTION: THE BIRTH PLACE
OF DADA. IN A WAY, HE IS RESPONSIBLE FOR STARTING ALL OF THIS. HE IS THE
ONE WHO GAVE ME AN EXHIBITION SPACE AND A PROBLEM TO SOLVE: MAKE AN
EXHIBITION ABOUT THE "REVOLUTION TO SMASH GLOBAL CAPITALISM." NOBODY
KNOWS WHAT WILL HAPPEN WHEN I AM GIVEN AN EXHIBITION SPACE AND A
PROBLEM TO SOLVE. HE WAS BRAVE ENOUGH TO DO IT. AS THE DIRECTOR OF A
CULTURAL INSTITUTION, HE HAS BEEN THINKING A LOT ABOUT MANAGEMENT
RECENTLY. HE TOLD ME HE WANTED TO WRITE SOMETHING ABOUT THE
MANAGEMENT OF CULTURAL PROJECTS. I THOUGHT, YES, THIS IS EXACTLY
WHAT WE NEED: DADA MANAGERS! WE WORKED TOGETHER ON THE TITLE.
I LIKED THE IDEA OF USING A HAND TO TELL THE STORY, SO I BORROWED
THE DEVICE TO ILLUSTRATE THE FIVE DESIGN PROBLEMS OF WORKING WITH
HYDROPONICS.

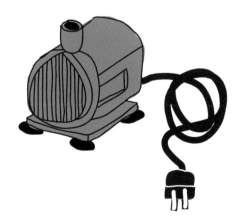

THE SLAP MANAGEMENT. NOTES FOR A MANIFESTO.

By Adrian Notz

Around the same time Antonio Scarponi started working on *Readykea*, the precursor to ELIOOO, for the exhibition *Dada New York II: The Revolution to Smash Global Capitalism* in Cabaret Voltaire, I started a coaching course in management in St. Gallen. I am learning a lot of models and instructions for all kinds of processes and a lot of "How to's" about management issues. One could also say, that I am learning conceptual devices about management. You can turn everything into a "conceptual device", to use a word that refers to Antonio's practice. This is especially true for ideas in management. You can use these models for anything in life, even to simply understand the world and be able to deal with it.

In this course, I learned that even a vision can be changed into a device: A vision is a star that you will never reach. I was told that a vision is like the north star which was used by sailors to navigate. To the sailors, it was also clear that they would never reach the star. This is how the management world understands a vision: It is totally necessary to have a vision, but you should never think you can actually reach it. If you can reach it, is not a vision, it is a goal. But before you do anything, you first need a vision.

For ELIOOO one could say the vision is that everybody will go to IKEA and build a device to grow food in their apartment. Of course the vision here is that everybody would use sustainable solutions to produce food right where they will consume it. One could say it very simply: Everybody would help save the planet and at the same time do something good for themselves. With this vision in mind, you can define a goal.

To describe and define a goal, I learned a very practical five point model for how to create a conceptual device of sorts. Like all models and manuals, it is very simple and it can be very easily explained by using the five fingers on your hand. It does not have an official name yet. *"The Five Finger Model To Define a Goal"* doesn't sound good, so I would like to use the name Antonio suggested: *The Slap Management Model*. With *The Slap Management Model* you can create five compartments into which you can categorize all the material you have. Also, by using *The Slap Management Model*, it is easier to transfer ideas and issues into other contexts. It's a way to put information into a different form, to put it into your hands, to physically grasp of it, to make it tangible and concrete like a slap.

I am going to apply *The Slap Management Model* to Antonio's ELIOOO and offer my own analysis.

The Thumb
I will start with the thumb. Only with the thumb can you grasp things properly and hold them. In The Slap Management Model, the thumb stands for the background and context of a pro-

ject. The background and context is an analysis of the starting situation, the context, and the potential of the project. Once you understand the background and context, you can then do a SWOT analysis. In a SWOT analysis, you analyse the Strengths and Weaknesses of the project and the Opportunities and Threats of the circumstances.

Looking at ELIOOO, we can say that the Strength is that it is simple to make, doesn't cost anything, is available more or less everywhere around the world, and it gives you a good feeling about what you're doing. The Weaknesses are that you might go out of town to buy the components at IKEA and that perhaps it doesn't really look very fancy. The Opportunities of ELIOOO are that we are in a time of global ecological consciousness. It is getting fashionable to get involved with saving the planet. It is even becoming mainstream to be involved in saving the planet. In this sense, using items from IKEA could also be an Opportunity. It is difficult to define Threats for ELIOOO that are not applicable to the whole world.

The Index Finger

Now I will move to the index finger. You normally use your index finger to point to things. In our model, the index finger stands for the goal of the project. I think that the goal of ELIOOO is to reach as many people as possible and show them how easy it can be to grow food at home and not worry about watering the plants as hydroponics technique suggests. The analysis of the context then can also show if this goal is realistic. By keeping it simple and by using IKEA, this goal seems to be realistic, this is what ELIOOO is all about.

The Middle Finger

The middle finger, sometimes referred to as the "fuck you" finger, stands for the development of a strategy. With its knock out attitude, it shows how you can reach the goal. It represents the master plan that defines the schedule, the people, the finances, the organization, and even the product that you need to reach the goal. ELIOOO hopes to reach its goal by using a "conceptual device", that is, a "how to" instruction as a product. On the product level, the master plan is quite easily defined: you do not need a lot of time to build ELIOOO, you can do it on your own, the costs are low, and it needs a minimum amount of organization. In a word, it is simple.

The Ring Finger

After you have defined a strategy, you realize the project. For the realization part we use the ring finger. The ring finger is normally used for the wedding ring, I use this to represent how a project is begun. With this function it indicates that things are becoming real and binding. When you start working on a project, you start spending money, moving goods, ordering people around, etc. You start to create! For this project, the first ELIOOOs have been created and the book you are reading has been published.

The Pinkie Finger

The only finger left is the pinkie finger. It doesn't really have a function, but because of its size, it can be seen as a questioning finger. In my model the pinkie stands for a monitoring system. The function of the monitoring system is to make sure you are still following the defined strategy. It also allows you to learn from the project. It is a moment to collect feedback and to check on the impact you are creating. Like the pinkie finger on your hand, it is not totally essential, but it is nice to have. It likes to connect with the thumb and it gets into places the other fingers don't.

ELIOOO was crowdfunded. IKEA is collaborating on this book. The ideas being published in this book will be realized by each reader who becomes a doer, a builder, a one-person factory. Together they will become a "crowd factory" of sustainable solutions. ELIOOO will be a realization of Antonio's conceptual device that suggests a paradigm shift and empowers people to grow their own food, to become the producers of an idea.

With the help of the five fingers, I have explained how ELIOOO is being realized. As it becomes more real, it threatens to make a real impact. Slap!

Adrian Notz (*1977, in Zurich) studied Art at the University of Art (HfK) in Bremen and Art Theory at the University of Fine Arts (ZHdK) in Zurich. From 2004 until 2006 he was curator, from 2006 co-director and from 2012 director of Cabaret Voltaire. Since 2010 he has been director of the faculty of Fine Arts at the school of visual arts in St. Gallen.

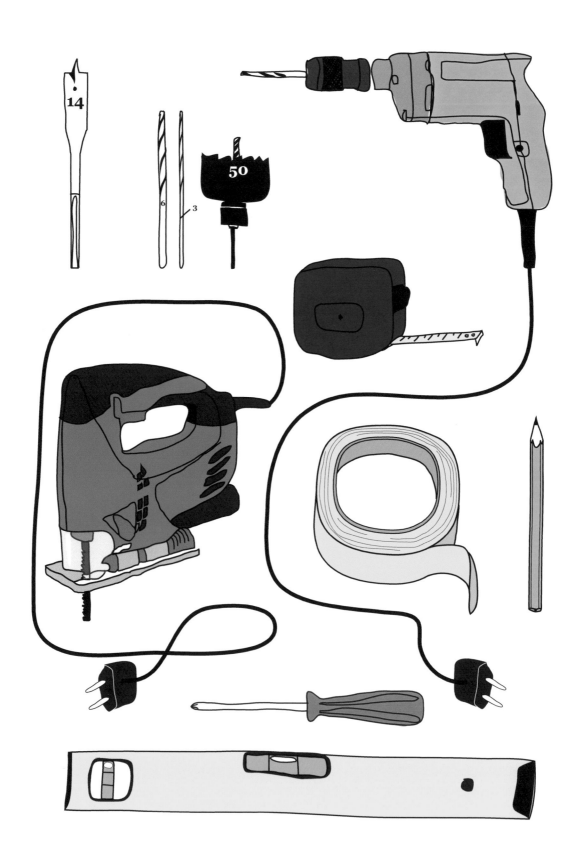

CPSIA information can be obtained at www.ICGtesting.com
Printed in the USA
LVIW01n1448100117
520451LV00011B/147